Also by Andrew Gilmore

The Last Lessons of Christ: Living by Faith in an Age of Despair

Walking with Christ: 30 Days with Jesus on the Road to Jerusalem

Under the Sun: Discover Your Calling and Live a Meaningful Life

Do No Work: Beat Burnout, Find Inner Peace, and Strengthen Your Faith by Studying the Most Overlooked of the Ten Commandments

YOUR UTMOST IS NOT ENOUGH

Trusting God Even When Life Doesn't Make Sense

Andrew Gilmore

Yours for free!
Transform your faith with these 12 habits.

Let's face it. Effective Christians can be annoying.

No matter what type of stress is going on in their lives, they always seem to handle it with grace and joy. Meanwhile, you're just lucky to make it to church on time. (Or is that just me?)

At times, effective Christians seem inhuman. Fake even. Yet the more you study them, the more you realize they are the real deal.

Imagine having a strong, healthy relationship with God. Imagine having peace in the midst of the storms of life. I've put together a free resource that will help you do just that.

The guide serves as a great companion to the book you're about to read. It's a super practical look at how to develop an effective faith.

Download this guide and find out how effective Christians live. Watch out, though. If you follow this advice, you just might become one too. Visit bit.ly/ttecd to grab your free copy.

Contents

Never Trust Theological Advice

I've written this same preface in other books, but the recommendation bears repeating here. Never trust theological advice. Charlatans, Scripture-twisters, and the just plain uninformed love to spew out advice to fill the mold of their worldview. Then they polish their plasters and present them as gospel.

Always approach sermons, Christian books, and any other form of theological advice with a critical eye—not in the disapproving sense of the word, but rather with discernment. I've done my best to present you with what I believe is the truth, but it is your responsibility to ensure I'm not some sort of crazy cult leader or communist. And even if I'm neither, I have biases I'm likely not even aware of. If you follow this advice not to trust my advice and suss out the truth for yourself, you will take ownership of your own faith. This can only be a good thing; too many Christians allow themselves to be spoon-fed the gospel without ever glancing at the ingredient list on the jar. We would all do well to study the jar.

Andrew Gilmore

The Mother of Disappointment

One of the most common questions both Christians and non-Christians ask is, "Why do bad things happen to good people?" It's a good question. But before answering, it is important to question the question itself.

Although you might be rolling your eyes right now, consider this before you check out. Jesus often asked questions in response to the questions people asked him. One example is the rich young man in Luke 18.[1] The man asked Jesus what he could do to inherit eternal life. Jesus's response? "Why do you call me good? No one is good except God alone" (v. 19). While Jesus didn't wait for an answer in this instance, he often did solicit responses from his questioners in order to reveal the deeper meaning behind their queries. Another example is in Mark 12, when some Pharisees tried to trick Jesus by asking whether or not they should pay taxes to Caesar. In response he asked two questions. First, "Why put me to the test?" (12:15). Jesus wanted to acknowledge out loud that his questioners' question was not an honest one, but rather a way to try and trick Jesus into saying something offensive. Here again Jesus didn't wait for an answer. But after being brought a Roman coin he asked his second question. "Whose likeness and inscription is this?" (12:16). When his questioners told him the coin bore Caesar's image, he said, "Render to Caesar the things that are Caesar's, and to God the things that are God's" (12:17). In asking the second question, Jesus forced his

---

[1] We also encounter the rich young man in Matthew 19 and Mark 10.

questioners to recognize that the currency they suggested withholding from Caesar bore the very image of Caesar. This acknowledgement led to a deeper spiritual axiom. We humans bear the image of God; therefore we belong to him.

Questioning questions and questioners has tremendous value in getting to the heart of the matter. In our case—why do bad things happen to good people?—it is valuable to know the worldview of the person behind the query. So the first question might be something like, "Do you believe there is a God?" If the answer is negative, then the question self-destructs, because a godless universe can have no absolute morals. That is, there are no "bad" things, just random, yet inevitable actions in a predetermined destiny. Likewise, there are no "good" people. We are simply a conglomeration of atoms, and emotions are nothing more than chemical reactions in the brain. Without any objective moral standard, feeding a hungry child has the same moral force as shooting one. Everything is neutral. For an atheist to say otherwise is, in my opinion, dishonest. Therefore, the question completely dissolves from the nontheistic point of view.[2] Instead of asking, "Why do bad things happen to good people?" the question becomes, "Why do things happen to people?" Not much of a question, is it?

But if you're reading this book, you're most likely a Christian, or at least sympathetic to the Christian worldview. Truth is, we could spend an entire book together answering this question, but a helpful question to ask the Christ-follower is, "Who do you consider good?" This sounds like a jerk move, but it's actually critical in order to frame the question in the proper perspective. After all, as we saw above, Jesus himself said, "No one is good but God alone." Does this mean

---

[2] I am, of course, painting atheists with broad strokes. Most would agree that shooting a child is wrong. That is not the question. The question is, on what basis can one say such an act is wrong?

people deserve the hideous evil that befalls them? Of course not. No child deserves leukemia. Young parents don't deserve miscarriages. Faithful men and women don't deserve a cheating partner, yet adultery happens every day. Nevertheless, God tells us through his prophet Isaiah that our righteousness is like filthy rags.[3] No matter how much good we do, the only one who is truly good is God.

Acknowledging this truth, we can see that what most Christians mean when they ask the above question is really something more like, "Why do bad things happen to *decent* people?" Decent people are those who try to do what is right, even though they stumble at times. So a corollary question arises: "Why don't all bad things happen to bad people?" Or maybe this: "Why do some bad people prosper while decent people suffer?" Analyzing the question in this manner helps us get to the heart of the matter. The question is really one of fairness. How is it fair that innocent children and godly men and women suffer illnesses, accidents, natural disasters, or worse—deliberate evil perpetrated by other individuals? How could God allow these things to happen?

Therefore, the question is born from a mismatch of expectation and reality. We expect that those who trust and follow God will prosper. We expect that those who read the Bible and pray will receive wisdom to anticipate when they are about to be swindled. We expect to reap what we sow. So when these expectations do not align with reality, we become disillusioned with life and, quite frankly, disappointed with God. As the saying goes, "Expectation is the mother of all disappointment."

---

[3] See Isaiah 64:6.

Two Types of Ills

At the risk of oversimplifying things, there are two types of "bad" things that occur: self-inflicted and externally inflicted. The first is more obvious: if you make bad decisions, bad things will happen. This happens to decent people all the time. One who has a habit of eating a pound of bacon every week will probably develop arterial blockage leading to cardiac arrest. One who texts while driving will probably experience some type of collision.

The converse is also true. Those who exercise regularly are more likely to live a longer, healthier life. Those who show up and work hard are more likely to get the promotion. Those who spend time with God will grow closer to him.

But what if you do everything right (or, at least, nothing wrong) and still fall? These are the externally inflicted evils. What if the other driver was texting her friend? What if the marathon runner still gets cancer and the lazy guy in the office gets promoted? This is the essence of the question, "Why do bad things happen to good people?" It is one born of expectations that we will reap what we sow. It is this disconnect between expectations and reality that this book aims to examine. What happens when we do everything right and yet still experience misfortune? If you're old enough to be able read this book, I can guarantee your life has been touched in some way by this disconnect.

Your Utmost for His Highest

In 1927, a woman named Gertrude "Biddy" Chambers published a collection of sermons and teachings written by her late husband, Oswald.[4] She titled the collection *My Utmost for His Highest*, a phrase

---

[4] See https://utmost.org/oswald-chambers-bio/ for more information.

she took from one of Oswald's sermons. While I confess I hadn't read it myself until I started working on this book, I loved the concept of the title: we give our best for God's glory, not for our own. But the truth of the matter is that our utmost, however good it is, is not enough. The book of Romans reminds us that all "fall short of the glory of God" (3:23). And on a practical level, we can give our utmost, care for orphans and widows, love our neighbors, spend time with God, and give generously and still experience untold tragedy. It happened to Job. It happened to Jesus. And it can happen to you too.

So what's the answer? Should we stop attempting to give our utmost, knowing such efforts are futile? Absolutely not. Remember those self-inflicted evils? Better ready your spare bedroom for them to settle into your life. If you sow stupid, you'll reap stupid. Living a godly life helps strengthen your faith so you can endure the storms life throws your way. If you knew a storm was coming, would you throw a party or board up your windows? If those reasons don't convince you, I believe it is a sin not to give your utmost. As the Scripture reads, "Whether you eat or drink, or whatever you do, do all to the glory of God" (1 Cor. 10:31).

The first part of this book is about giving your all for God. It is about living with integrity and establishing rock-solid habits that promote the growth of your faith and knowledge of the Lord. Part II deals with the fallout of doing all these things yet still suffering. How does that make sense? How is that fair?

Last, part III looks at the example Jesus set of how to balance these disparities in our lives—that of doing good, but receiving bad. If anyone has experience with these things, it is our Lord.

Oh, and lest you think I'm ducking the original question at the beginning of this section, I'll do my best to answer it. While we'll address the question in greater detail in part II, the bottom line is that we take eternity out of the picture when posing the question.

Yes, we will suffer needlessly, but everything will be restored in heaven. Yes, enemies of God will receive their due, but it may not be until the final judgment. Remember what Paul wrote? "I consider that the sufferings of this present time are not worth comparing with the glory that is to be revealed to us" (Rom. 8:18). Compared to the glory and restoration God will provide, the suffering of this world is but a mere scratch.

Part I

For God's Sake Be Excellent!

CHAPTER 1

How to Wage War against Your Thermodynamic Body of Death

*If your theory is found to be against the Second Law of
Thermodynamics I can give you no hope; there is nothing for it but to
collapse in deepest humiliation.*[5]
—Arthur Stanley Eddington

Your brain is lazy. So trick it.

If someone asked you to make a list of the most essential habits of
the Christian life, undoubtedly you would include two items:
reading the Scriptures and prayer. These inclusions would elicit
little controversy except among the fringes of Christianity. Put simply,
studying the Word and praying are foundational to an effective
Christian life. Those who argue against these things often cite people
they know who engage in these activities yet don't embody the
Christian life; people who have a good knowledge of the Bible but are
rude, petty, stingy, or lazy. I have no doubt these people exist, because

---

[5] Arthur Stanley Eddington, *The Nature of the Physical World* (London:
Cambridge University Press, 1948), PDF version, 37. Retrieved from
https://henry.pha.jhu.edu/Eddington.2008.pdf.

I know some personally. In fact, I see one every day when I brush my teeth. So please hear me on this: I'm not saying Christians should only read the Bible. That's how Pharisees and Judaizers develop. What I *am* saying is that knowledge of the Scriptures and prayer are essential components of the effective Christian walk. The best example of this is none other than Jesus Christ himself. He knew the Jewish Tanakh (what we call the Old Testament) forward and backward. The Gospel writers recorded dozens of instances in which Jesus quoted from the Scriptures. These quotations were often spontaneous in response to testing or temptation, demonstrating that our Lord had these passages memorized. As for prayer, the Gospels also record numerous instances in which Jesus snuck away to pray. So if prayer and knowledge of the Scriptures were important to Jesus, they should be important to Christians too. Again, this isn't some huge controversy—the majority of Christians agree on the importance of these practices—but you'd be surprised at the number of people with negative attitudes toward these disciplines.

Despite near-universal agreement on the importance of such habits, few of us actually do these things on a daily basis. In fact, according to research by LifeWay, only 28% of Americans who identify as Christians systematically read the Bible every day.[6][7] Where is the disconnect? Are we all just horrible Christians? Are we just plain hypocrites? There may be some hypocrisy going around, but I think there's a deeper issue here. Let's talk about thermodynamics.

---

[6] Bob Smietana, "LifeWay Research: Americans Are Fond of the Bible, Don't Actually Read It," Lifeway Research, April 25, 2017, https://lifewayresearch.com/2017/04/25/lifeway-research-americans-are-fond-of-the-bible-dont-actually-read-it/.

[7] *American Views on Bible Reading: Representative Survey of 1000 Americans*, April 1, 2017, distributed by LifeWay Research, http://lifewayresearch.com/wp-content/uploads/2017/04/Sept-2016-American-Views-Bible-Reading.pdf, slide 23.

The Second Law of Thermodynamics and You!

Have you ever heard of the heat death of the universe? Sounds like a cheery subject, doesn't it? The Heat Death theory predicts that at some time in the future, the universe will reach thermodynamic equilibrium. Or, in English, the universe will run out of usable energy; motion will cease and all bodies will rest at the same temperature. Physicists base this theory on the second law of thermodynamics. But before we go there, let's briefly explain the first law.

Now, you may not think you know much about thermodynamics, but even if you've never picked up a physics textbook, we all instinctively understand these laws. I won't pretend to be a physicist, but here's how I understand the first and second laws. (There are four total, from zero to three, but my brain might explode if I attempt to explain all four.)

The first law deals with the conservation of energy, which sounds neat and like a good idea, but really all it means is that energy cannot be created or destroyed, just transferred. So running a race requires calories, which we get from food. Plants and animals from which we derive said calories rely on the energy of the sun—plants for photosynthesis, and animals that eat those plants. Bottom line: it is impossible to manufacture energy without consuming energy at the same time.

This is important as we set up the second law, which states that the entropy in a closed system will never decrease. Say what? Another way to state it is that energy always moves from a concentrated state to a scattered state. One common definition of entropy is the measure of a system's disorder.[8] So if you place an ice cube in a glass

---

[8] Merriam-Webster, s.v. "entropy," accessed April 5, 2021, https://www.merriam-webster.com/dictionary/enropy.

of hot water, you've got energy neatly arranged: all of the warm molecules in the liquid H_2O and all of the cold molecules stored in the ice cube. But what happens as time passes? The second law of thermodynamics tells us that entropy always increases, which means our neatly ordered energy will spread out as the heat flows to the cold and melts the ice. Once this process is complete, the glass will achieve thermodynamic equilibrium, leaving us with a warm cup of water. But why do we never see the reverse? Why is it that when we drop an ice cube in a warm cup of water, the water never gets hotter while the ice cube gets colder? It is because entropy is always increasing as defined by the second law of thermodynamics.

Another way to think of the second law is like this. Usable energy is always being converted into unusable energy. Once the glass of water is at equilibrium, to heat up or cool down the water would require an input of energy into the system. This is because energy is only useful when it's grouped together, as we see in the ice water example. Energy flows from the hot water to the ice until it is spread out. So to heat up lukewarm water, we would have to use a microwave, the stove, or direct sunlight—adding energy to the system.

We can also think of entropy in terms of probability. One time, during my high school years in Nevada, my maternal grandparents flew in to Reno from Oklahoma City for a visit. The Tilleys are competitive folk, so it wasn't long after they settled in and shrugged off the jet lag that we began playing games. The domino is their favorite competitive medium, but on this particular day we broke out five dice for a game of Greedy. There exists, I'm told, several iterations of this game with various names attached to them, but if you've never played Greedy, here's the gist. A player rolls five dice and scores points for every one and five rolled, setting aside those dice. Ones are worth 100 points. Fives are worth fifty. You may pick up the remaining non-scoring dice and roll them, but if you fail to roll a one or a five, your turn is over and you lose all the points you accumulated during that turn. In other words, you got greedy. So, for example, if I roll all five dice and get two ones and one five, I can quit and keep the points or pick up the two non-scorers and reroll them. Say I roll one five and one two. I set the five aside and then decide again whether to quit or pick up the two and reroll it. The fewer dice you have remaining, the less likely you are to roll a one or a five. You get the idea. First to 10,000 points wins.

When I play this game, I am greedy. I will pick up one or two dice and continue rolling even with thousands of points on the line. This particular day was no exception, and I was losing pretty badly. I was down by a couple thousand points as Granny, Papa, and the rest of my family inched closer to 10,000. But I should interject an additional rule of the game. I'm not sure if this is an official regulation or simply a tradition passed down, but we've always played that if, at any time, a player rolls five ones in a single roll, that player instantly wins the game. So about halfway through the game, when it had become apparent I wasn't going to win, I announced to the group I was going to roll five ones. As I got further behind with each turn, I turned up the braggadocio a notch until it reached fever pitch. Or, as my mom likes to tell the story, "You were being so annoying." (I know that's quite difficult to fathom, but apparently she wasn't the only one to share in this opinion.)

I knew rolling five ones was unlikely, but it was fun to see my competitors' reactions to my overconfidence. Like I said, games are serious business in my family; if you're not first, you might as well be last, so any perception of failing to take a game seriously broke the code of honor. Well aware of this subtext, I enjoyed pushing the envelope with my blasé attitude. It was a game within a game, transforming a simple dice game into a psychological chess match of wills.

As the game wound down, my turn came up. I picked up the dice with much pomp but little circumstance and flicked my wrist like a high roller at the Golden Nugget. As the dice came to rest, the room fell silent for a brief instant as we all surveyed the improbability at hand.

I rolled five ones.

I leapt from my chair in elation and ran out of the room like I had just become the next contestant on *The Price Is Right*. This was beyond unlikely. It was like a pitcher hitting a walk-off grand slam in game seven of the World Series. (Okay, maybe not that unlikely, but that's how it felt.)

Thanks to the wonders of mathematics, we can calculate the probability of rolling five ones. Consider rolling one die. The chances of rolling a one are one out of six, since there are six sides. But what are the chances of rolling a one two times in a row? Individually, each roll is one in six, so we multiply the two probabilities since one outcome is dependent on the other, meaning the chance of rolling two ones decreases to one in thirty-six. What about with another die? The odds of rolling a third one decrease by another factor of six, leaving us with 1/216 odds. Five ones in a row? 1/7,776.

Let's go back to our glass of ice water. For the heat to remain in the water and the ice to stay cold, it would be a bit like rolling five ones, because such an arrangement of energy is just one of many possible arrangements. But rather than just 7,776 possible outcomes, there are over one septillion molecules of water in a single glass![9] That's one followed by twenty-four zeros! So having the energy in our glass to be neatly arranged by hot and cold molecules is such a statistical improbability that it would never happen. It is also helpful

---

[9] One mole of water (about eighteen milliliters) contains 6.022×10^{23} molecules of H_2O. Assuming 200 milliliters for a glass of water, you get almost seven septillion molecules.

to think about entropy in the reverse: a lukewarm glass of water would never spontaneously form ice cubes. Why not? Because of the second law of thermodynamics.

Combining the principles undergirding the first and second laws of thermodynamics we get, simply, that the amount of energy in the universe is fixed and the amount of usable energy is always decreasing. I said at the onset that we all intuitively understand these laws, even if our understanding is only subconscious. Here's what I mean.

Your body is kind of like a machine. It's efficient, but the amount of useable energy it contains is always decreasing. Without adding energy (i.e. food) to the system, you'll eventually run out of energy and die. This is common sense, but what if the second law also applies to behavior? For example, it is very unlikely that someone would spontaneously read her Bible. Because entropy is always increasing, it is almost impossible for such an act to happen on its own. It would be like an ice cube in hot water that never melts. The only way to achieve this result is by introducing work into the system. The problem is, your brain hates work and actively rebels against it. Why?

It's a matter of survival.

In order to do any kind of work—exercise, laundry, fishing, or even thinking—you burn calories. And if you run out of calories, as we've established, you die. The instinctual side of your brain knows this on a deep level, and it's doing everything it can to ensure its own survival. Therefore, it rebels against work as much as possible in order to preserve energy. Think about it. What is the average person more likely to do: read a book or watch a movie? All things being equal, the movie almost always wins out. The reasons for this are myriad, but I believe the most important factor is energy usage. While both are forms of entertainment, reading requires active participation while movies convert viewers into passive zombies. So naturally, your brain prefers watching because it's easier. The question, then, is how does anything requiring effort ever get done?

One answer is endorphins. Certain types of "work," like exercise, cause your brain to release endorphins, which make you feel good. This creates a reward system in your brain, which makes you more okay with running that 5K since you know that you'll be rewarded in the end.

The second answer is also obvious. We are more than just the instinctual animals that that part of our brain represents, and we are able to make rational, logical decisions and think about long-term consequences. Example: If I save for retirement, I might not have to rely on the government to take care of me when I'm elderly. I won't even pretend to understand the brain, but from experience I can say one thing: the animalistic side of our brains has more power over us than we would probably care to admit.

Let's go back to the second law of thermodynamics. Entropy tells us that the most likely scenario will occur: a hot cup of coffee will lose heat over time as it sits on the countertop. The only way for it to get hotter? To add energy (work) to it: put it in the microwave, for example. But how does this apply to you and me?

Here's a simple example: tying your shoe. The second law of thermodynamics suggests that shoelaces don't spontaneously tie themselves. It is way more likely that a tied shoe would become untied than for an untied shoe to form itself into a bow. Therefore, in order to reduce entropy (i.e. reduce disorder), we must introduce work into the system. Remember, a core part of your brain hates work because it understands that doing work requires calories and calories are finite. But another part of you knows you must tie your shoes or you will trip and fall. So what does your brain do? It begrudgingly complies with logic, but does its best to conserve energy. How does it do so? By creating a habit.

Think about it. Whether you realize it or not, I bet you always tie the same shoe first. Some might tie the right first, some might tie the left first, but I can almost guarantee that whichever it is, you tie the same shoe first every time. Furthermore, you probably always tie them in the same manner, even if it's been a long time since you wore shoes with laces. True, most everyone uses the basic bowknot, but even still, the methods vary slightly: how tightly you tie it, which finger you use to hold down the laces while forming the bow, or whether you use a single or double knot.

Why is this the case? Your brain establishes these techniques, these habits, in order to conserve energy. Tasks you do every day can be routinized by your brain to the point where they are as efficient as possible. I can barely do any two things at the same time, but I can have a conversation and tie my shoes at the same time. Nevertheless, I can assure you this wasn't the case when I was still learning to tie shoelaces—that is, before I developed the habit.

Understanding this principle can help us leverage a hidden superpower of our brains in order to establish important habits in our lives, like reading the Bible and praying. By creating a system which requires little thought or friction, we can make things like exercise and reading so automatic, we feel off if we *don't* do them.

So you see, I don't believe Christians fail to read the Bible because they are terrible, two-faced hypocrites, but rather because a large part of their brains is actively fighting against them doing so. (And this doesn't even take into account Satan and the powers of darkness at play, doing everything in their power to separate us from God.) Remember what Paul wrote to the Romans?

> *I do not understand my own actions. For I do not do what I want, but I do the very thing I hate. . . . For I know that*

nothing good dwells in me, that is, in my flesh. For I have the desire to do what is right, but not the ability to carry it out. For I do not do the good I want, but the evil I do not want is what I keep on doing. Now if I do what I do not want, it is no longer I who do it, but sin that dwells within me.

So I find it to be a law that when I want to do right, evil lies close at hand. For I delight in the law of God, in my inner being, but I see in my members another law waging war against the law of my mind and making me captive to the law of sin that dwells in my members. Wretched man that I am! Who will deliver me from this body of death? Thanks be to God through Jesus Christ our Lord! So then, I myself serve the law of God with my mind, but with my flesh I serve the law of sin.

Romans 7:15, 18–25

So if even Paul, one of the most influential Christians in history and author of close to a third of the New Testament, can struggle with these issues, anyone can. So what's the solution? Is there any hope for bags of flesh like us? Fortunately, being aware of things like the second law of thermodynamics and their human corollaries is a great step in overcoming them. One solution, you'll see, involves gym showers and making your bed.

Your Best Counterattack to Entropy

One of the most poignant things I've ever read from author Seth Godin is his advice on establishing a habit of working out at a gym. We've all heard of people who start a New Year's resolution to lose weight and get in shape, so they join their local gym on January 1. By February 1, they may still have the membership, but feel guilty that they never go. By March or maybe April, they've canceled their membership. In fact, a Harris survey revealed that among those who quit the gym within one year, 18% bailed before March.[10]

Godin's advice, though, leverages the power of habit. Here's what he recommends: "The way to get in shape is to go to the gym every single day, change your clothes and take a shower. If you can do that every single day for a month, pretty soon you'll start doing something while you're there."[11] How bizarre. How does this help someone get in shape? Mr. Godin has figured out what most people who achieve goals have discovered: when you make something a habit, you're more likely to succeed.

There is absolutely no friction, no mental block from your brain in simply driving to the gym and taking a shower. These are things your brain has already mastered if you've been driving and showering for any amount of time. You've already developed a habit. (By the way, just as with your shoelaces, I bet you have a routine when you shower that you do the same way every time). Because there is no friction here, no promise of inefficient work, the more primitive sides of our brains assent to the task. Meanwhile, the gym member is tricking his brain into establishing a habit of going to the gym. Once that habit is in place, it would seem weird and out of place to not go to the gym. Once you're there, you might as well work out. You are paying good money, after all.

The habit is our best counterattack to the second law of thermodynamics and the resultant complaint from our brains against work. By nature, all work is inefficient and burns precious calories, but by coddling the primitive sides of our brains, we can overcome

---

[10] "New Year's Fitness Goals Survey," Coupon Cabin, January 3, 2013, https://www.couponcabin.com/blog/new-years-fitness-goals-survey/.

[11] Seth Godin, "Crash Diets and Good Habits," Seth's Blog, August 12, 2012, https://seths.blog/2012/08/crash-diets-and-good-habits/.

many of these self-inflicted objections and allow logic and willpower to have some say. If you tell yourself you're just going to the gym for a shower, you are more likely to go. But getting there is often the main point of resistance, so once you're there, it's not too difficult to hop on an elliptical for a few minutes. Take that, entropy! And yet, if you really want to lose weight, may I suggest reading your Bible?

Want to Lose Weight? Read Your Bible

Do you make your bed every day? I don't. But maybe I should. Not because spreading out sheets and blankets is morally right or because smoothing out your comforter does anything for your soul. But maybe, just maybe, it does something to your brain. Making your bed every morning gives you what is known as a "small win"— something easy that's quickly accomplished. When you get a small win, you're more likely to accomplish complex tasks throughout the day. People who develop habits like these are generally more productive than those who don't.[12]

So why don't I make my bed every day? If I know it's good for me, why don't I take the few minutes to adjust the pillows and reset the sheets? It's simple: I haven't made it a habit.

Why Some Habits Matter More Than Others

In addition to the small win, another important concept is the "keystone habit"—a habit that influences other decisions in your life. I came across the idea in Charles Duhigg's book *Power of Habit: Why We Do What We Do in Life and Business*. Here's what Duhigg has to say:

---

[12] See, for example, Charles Duhigg, *The Power of Habit: Why We Do What We Do in Life and Business* (New York: Random House, 2012), Kindle edition, location 1760 of 6093.

> *Some habits, in other words, matter more than others in remaking businesses and lives. These are "keystone habits," and they can influence how people work, eat, play, live, spend, and communicate. Keystone habits start a process that, over time, transforms everything.*[13]

That includes how much you weigh.

Duhigg reports that behavioral psychologists and other scientists noticed that people who developed a keystone habit in one area of their lives tended to make better decisions in other, unrelated areas of their lives.

Take finances, for example. As pure anecdotal evidence, money management expert and radio show host Dave Ramsey likes to mention that people intent on getting out of debt also tend to lose weight during the process. Maybe that just means they're eating out less often. But what if it's more than that? Doing something important in one area of our lives often helps us make better decisions in other areas too. Keystone habits work to change who you are at a fundamental level, and I can't think of a better habit than reading your Bible and praying to God. Can you?

But that's not a small win. Reading the Bible takes mental acuity and time. It's too hard! I can't do that!

Why make it complicated? What if we combined the small win and the keystone habit? What if you committed to reading just one chapter of the Bible every day, no matter what? What if you decided to pray to God for two minutes after that? Easy, right? In doing so, you'd get the small win that would start your day off right and, over time, develop that keystone habit that just might shed some pounds from your waistline.

---

[13] Ibid., location 1596 of 6093.

Hear me on this: starting a spiritual discipline with the motivation to lose weight is just stupid. So don't do that. But if you develop the most important habit—spending time with God—then the side effects can only be positive. Jesus said it better than I ever could: "Seek first the kingdom of God and his righteousness, and all these things will be added to you" (Matt. 6:33). Do you believe that?

Fighting against universal laws of physics sounds like a bad idea; you'll always lose. We humans are bound by the laws of time and space. Our bodies are subject to illness, fatigue, decay, and entropy. But here's the good news: we are much more than just our physical bodies. God created us in his image and gave us minds and souls. To attempt to overcome the limitations of the flesh by sheer willpower is silly. Rather, we can turn to the limitless Almighty for comfort, aid, and motivation. Only God can help us transcend our bodies of death, so we must seek him first. He is our source of hope and life. But with a foundation of healthy habits, we are much more likely to make wise decisions in pursuit of our utmost for God's highest.

CHAPTER 2
Spiritual Scurvy and Pagan Babble

The only people who achieve much are those who want knowledge so badly that they seek it while the conditions are still unfavourable. Favourable conditions never come.
—C. S. Lewis[14]

Some practical advice for spending time with God.

Assenting to the importance of spiritual discipline is not enough. Perhaps you've done that but still struggle with finding time to spend with God. Maybe you're a physicist who can tell me all the ways I butchered my explanation and application of the second law of thermodynamics, but you still falter when it comes to disorder in your spiritual life. Maybe you're a behavioral psychologist, but you still struggle with habits and willpower. Or maybe, just maybe, you're a born-again Christian who can't seem to find time for Christ. No judgment here. I struggle every day.

Before we proceed, I want to reemphasize that reading the Bible and prayer are not the alphas and omegas of Christian living. I know

---

[14] C. S. Lewis, *The Weight of Glory: And Other Addresses* (New York: HarperCollins, 2009), Kindle edition, 61.

plenty of people, including myself, who read a chapter or two of Scripture, pray for a few minutes, check the boxes off of their to-do lists, and move on with their days, forgetting about what they read that morning and ignoring what God was trying to tell them. I bring this up only to remind you that these two tasks should not become ends in themselves, but rather should be a vehicle for honoring God with your life.

Nevertheless, these two disciplines are keystone habits that can transform everything about your being. How is this possible? The mistake that many well-meaning Christians make is assuming that this transformation comes from the tasks in and of themselves. Truth is, if you do these things on a regular basis, it is possible to become a more disciplined person but never grow closer to Christ, the same as if you established a habit of exercising every morning. Real, lasting transformation comes only through the power of Jesus Christ. What's the difference between a Christian who reads the Bible and prays every morning and a Muslim who reads the Quran and prays to Allah every day?

The difference is this:

> *For the word of God is living and active, sharper than any two-edged sword, piercing to the division of soul and of spirit, of joints and of marrow, and discerning the thoughts and intentions of the heart.*
> Hebrews 4:12

You see, when you study the living Bible and pray to the one true God, he can provide transformation. These activities, then, are means rather than ends. They are means to grow closer to God, discern his will for your life, and experience transformation. When approaching quiet time with God with the goal of honoring him, I guarantee you won't be disappointed with the results.

And yet, despite all of this, there are times when we struggle. Times we lack motivation. Times when we are tempted to forsake Bible reading and prayer. Even if you've already developed a habit, these moments will come. So what do we do?

What to Do When You Don't Enjoy the Bible

Perhaps we should start with a different question and then work our way back to the Bible. What do you do when you don't enjoy vitamin C? Answer: you get scurvy.

I use this line quite a bit on my son Damian, the pickiest eater I've ever met. As I write this, he is progressing and getting better, as I always thought he would, but at age twelve, it has taken longer than anticipated. These are the foods he eats: jelly, goldfish (the cracker, not the animal), and milk. I think that's it. Yes, I realize milk is not a food, but I wanted to pad the list. But if that wasn't extreme enough, he will only drink *skim* milk and only eat *grape* jelly and *regular* goldfish. Get out of here with those flavor-blasted fish. Pure nonsense. I won't pick on him too much; we all have our foibles, and there are way worse vices than grape jelly. Imagine what the Twinkie parents have to deal with. (Yeah, I'm pretty sure he doesn't like Twinkies.)

Occasionally, Katie and I will require Damian to eat a fruit or vegetable with dinner. When he complains, I enjoy telling him, "Son, we don't want you to get scurvy!" Or, if I'm feeling extra dramatic, "We love you too much to let you die!" He loves it when I say those things.

The truth is, scurvy is a nasty condition. Made famous by pirates and sailors, the disease is caused by a lack of vitamin C. Did you know those afflicted with scurvy can bleed from their gums? How terrible is that? In addition, scurvy causes fatigue, personality changes, limb and joint pain, hair loss, and even death. Want to know the treatment? Eat an orange. Fresh produce is the best way to obtain the vitamin, but most fruits and veggies don't last more than a week or two before spoiling. Since sailors could be at sea for months, they did not have access to what they needed to stave off the disease.

Often, you and I are just like Damian when it comes to the Christian life—at risk of spiritual scurvy. We'd rather bleed from our gums than pick up a Bible.

God and his Word are inseparable, so you can't despise the Scriptures and love God. As Jesus said, "Heaven and earth will pass away, but my words will not pass away" (Matt. 24:35). But if you're struggling, I get where you're coming from. I just slogged through Ezekiel, and I did not enjoy it. Me, the Bible author guy. I don't remember it being such a tough book, but I fell asleep several times while reading it. In other moments, my mind wandered: *How will I market my new book? How much milk is in the fridge?* Anything to take my mind off of Ezekiel.

It's funny that this is the first wall I've hit since starting at Genesis several months ago. It used to be that I would get bogged down in Leviticus—the third book in the Bible. Then it was First Chronicles. Then it was Psalms. Then Isaiah. Every time I reread the Bible, I seem to progress further in the text before I hit the mental wall. For you, I'm sure it's no different.

I will give you some practical advice, but you've probably heard it before. The first key is one of motivation. Just like with any goal, you must own the "why" behind it. If your goal is to run a marathon because your friend wants to do it and needs a companion, you're way less likely to put in the necessary miles to achieve that goal. If you want to lose weight because someone else thinks you weigh too much, good luck with that one. Similarly, if you attempt a quiet time regimen because you feel pressured by your pastor or small group, you're not going to succeed. You must believe that reading the Scriptures and praying are some of the best things you can do for your spiritual life. You have to own the importance of the activities. Again, it goes back to "Why?" Why do you want to spend time in the Word and in prayer? Is it for peer approval or is it to grow closer to God day by day? If it's the former, you'll fall away. But the motivation behind the latter will carry you for the rest of your life.

The second key is consistency. It's better to read for five minutes every day than for sixty minutes one day a week. The total amount you read is more in the latter scenario (sixty minutes vs. thirty-five), but you go six days in between encounters with the Word. (Try eating all your calories for the week on Sunday and tell me how that works out.) Just like we discussed in chapter one, habits are the best way to overcome the brain's resistance to expending energy.

Here are some other tips:

Pray that God will give you a love for his Word. When you struggle in any area of your life, where's the best place to turn? To God, of course. Jesus said, "Blessed are those who hunger and thirst for righteousness, for they shall be satisfied" (Matt. 5:6). He will amaze you with his response to this request. God loves few things more than saying "yes" to those who petition him with righteous requests. Even those who already read and study the Bible need to pray this prayer from time to time.

Read Psalm 119. God called David a man after his own heart for a reason.[15] Sure, David messed up plenty: Bathsheba and the census and all that. But despite those things, David loved God's Word, and that's what Psalm 119 is about. It's an acrostic—each stanza begins

---

[15] See Acts 13:22.

with a different letter of the Hebrew alphabet. Reading through it will give you a different perspective on Scripture and a model for what it looks like to delight in God's Word.

Cultivate a reading habit. We've already discussed habits a bit, and I've written about it elsewhere too, so I won't belabor the point. But a great shortcut to forming a habit is to use a trigger—something that immediately precedes the desired habit. For me, it's getting out of bed (after some coffee, of course), but you don't have to do it first thing in the morning. It could be first thing when you get home from work, or immediately after dinner, or immediately after brushing your teeth . . . you get the idea. The trigger has to be something you do every day in order to be effective. In essence, you're piggybacking off of other habits you've already formed. This could even be something as simple as setting an alarm on your phone for the same time every day as a reminder to spend time with God.

Find another format. I prefer reading, but audio is a no less valid way to consume the Scriptures. In reality, the majority of people throughout history consumed God's Word by listening rather than reading. Only the elite or precious few had the luxury of learning to read. This is why Jesus often said to the crowds, "You have heard it said" before quoting Scripture.[16] But to the religious leaders he would ask, "Have you never read?" The Pharisees and scribes read and studied the Scriptures. In the twenty-first century, countless audio resources abound. Whether podcast or audiobook, the opportunities to listen to the Word of God have never been greater. My son Thomas isn't a big reader, so we sometimes listen to the Bible on the way to school in the morning.

Regardless of how you consume God's Word, when you commit

---

[16] For example, see the Sermon on the Mount. In Matthew chapter 5, Jesus says, "You have heard that it was said" five times.

to the Bible, you will have moments of clarity, fulfillment, and gratification, but you'll also have moments of boredom and fatigue. That's normal. Take, for instance, Ezekiel 45:14 (NIV): "The prescribed portion of olive oil, measured by the bath, is a tenth of a bath from each cor (which consists of ten baths or one homer, for ten baths are equivalent to a homer)." Or how about 1 Kings 7:24? "Under [the brim of the molten sea] were gourds, for ten cubits, compassing the sea all around. The gourds were in two rows, cast with it when it was cast." I almost fell asleep just now. I mean, does it really matter how many baths are in a homer? Or how many gourds adorn the sea? Maybe. Maybe not. But unless you dive in, you'll never know. But whatever you do, please don't get spiritual scurvy. Persevere. You'll be glad you did.

One Aspect of Prayer You Might Not Have Considered (But Probably Should)

I hesitate to write this to you, because I'm not very good at what I'm about to recommend. But although it might sound obvious, in practice (for me, at least) it's difficult. What is it?

Listening.

A few years ago, Katie and I bought walkie-talkies for our children for Christmas. When I saw the radios on the shelf in a sporting goods store, I became a kid again for a few moments. I imagined all of the possibilities for fun and adventure that came with these devices. And when I read on the package that the range was up to two miles, I was sold. Two miles might as well be 100 to an eight-year-old.

If you've ever used a walkie-talkie, you know you must press and hold the transmit button so the other radio can receive your message. The catch is that while you're holding down your button, you cannot receive any transmissions from your friend. Being used to cell phones and tablet video calls, my children did not understand this concept. My youngest son was continuously holding down the button and wondering why his sister never responded to his chatter. So I told him, "You have to let go of the button when you're not talking, or else you'll never hear a response."

I think prayer can be like those walkie-talkies. We ask and beg and praise and extol, but we never take our finger off the button to see what God has to say in return. We're too busy talking. My daughter wasn't silent; she was responding to my son's radio calls, but he couldn't hear what she had to say because he never let go of the button.

Let me be the first to raise my hand and say, "I've never heard an audible voice of God." Although he has spoken to people like Moses and Adam and Eve in this manner, God doesn't seem to speak to us in this way anymore. It's not that he can't, but rather that he chooses not to. Why not? Only he can fully answer that question, but I think there are some clues.

First, God has already spoken to us in the form of the Law of Moses, the prophets, and his very own incarnation, Jesus Christ. In other words, the Bible is the primary way God communicates to us. That's why it is so critical to read and understand it. I believe God spoke directly to people in the ancient world because they did not yet have the Scriptures. Abram couldn't have picked up a Bible. Moses didn't have the book of Genesis to refer to. In fact, tradition holds that he *wrote* Genesis! These men and many more men and women lived out the Scriptures we have today.

Second, God wants to leave an element of faith in the equation. Why do this? Why withhold ironclad proof? God wants us to *choose* a relationship with him; he's not going to force it. *But if he would speak to us, wouldn't we be more likely to believe?* Possibly yes, but even that wouldn't be enough for some people. How do I know? Look no further than the Old Testament. God spoke directly to the Israelites when he gave them the Ten Commandments. As Moses recounted in Deuteronomy, "These words the LORD spoke to all your assembly at the mountain out of the midst of the fire, the cloud, and the thick darkness, with a loud voice; and he added no more" (5:22). After delivering the Ten Commandments, God sent the Israelites back to their tents while Moses went up into the "thick darkness" to receive the rest of the law (Ex. 20:21). With Moses gone over a month, the people became restless and afraid and demanded that Aaron make them gods. Just forty days prior, they had heard the very voice of God, and yet they were unable to place their trust in him. Instead, they let fear rule over them, and in the process they broke the first two of the ten commandments God had just given Moses. So you see, even those who heard God's audible voice struggled with faith. Regardless, there's a difference between believing he exists and wanting a relationship with him, which leads us to the next point.

Third, God judges in proportion to the amount of revelation he gives us. Therefore, those who have the most evidence and yet do not respond accordingly will receive the harshest judgment. The apostle Paul wrote that because of the magnificence of creation, people are "without excuse" when it comes to knowing God exists. Nevertheless, some people receive more evidence than others regarding the existence and nature of God. But on those who receive these revelations, God will impose a higher standard. Let's go back to the Old Testament for a minute. People often see the God of the Old Testament as vindictive or excessively harsh, but you've got to realize that if humans in general have no excuse for discerning knowledge of God, the Israelites had even less of an excuse. God spoke directly to them at first. He performed miracles in Egypt and in the wilderness. He gave them the Law. He sent prophet after prophet to correct the people. Yet the people turned their hearts from him time and again. As a result, God punished the Israelites in kind. He gave them every kind of opportunity and evidence they needed to obey, but they often refused.

Think of it this way. Suppose you had a child who took a cookie from a jar in your kitchen and ate it before dinner. Would it be fair to punish her if you had never told her not to do so? But what if you had told her several times not to take a cookie without asking first? What if you taped a note to the jar (assuming the child could read, of course) that read, "You must have permission before eating a cookie," then placed the jar on an out-of-reach shelf? If your child grabbed a stepladder, climbed it, grabbed the jar, tore off the note, reached in, and ate a cookie, would it be unfair to discipline the child? Of course not. Therefore, if God were to broadcast himself to all people everywhere, he would have to respond in kind to those who still reject him. Instead, as Peter wrote, God is "patient toward you, not wishing that any should perish, but that all should reach repentance" (2 Pet. 3:9). As a result, God uses more subtle ways to reveal himself to provide humanity every opportunity to turn to him. Nevertheless, when God deems the time right, Jesus will return like a flash of lightning to judge the living and the dead.[17] Some people, no matter how much evidence they receive, will still choose to reject the Lord.

Last, God uses various other means to communicate to us. We've already discussed the Bible, but God reveals himself in many other ways. One way he speaks is through the majesty of his creation. David wrote, "The heavens declare the glory of God, and the sky above proclaims his handiwork" (Ps. 19:1). The magnificence and grandeur of our natural world lends itself to an intelligent designer so much that one must repress evidence to deny the existence of God.

---

[17] See Matthew 24:27 and Acts 10:42.

Another method is morality. Every human in every type of culture knows that torturing other humans is wrong. That's not up for debate. Everyone everywhere knows that stealing is wrong. Those who claim otherwise are lying. How do I know? They will sing a different tune if subjected to torture or theft themselves. These are extreme examples, but they represent a universal morality written on the hearts of humanity.[18] This revelation demonstrates the heart and character of God, because without a god, objective moral values cannot exist.

Yet another method of communication is other people. God uses ministers, friends, elders, children, and others to reveal truth about himself. Many years ago, my former pastor, Dustin, encouraged people to text him questions that he would answer after the service. I asked why Jesus cried at Lazarus's tomb if he knew he was going to resurrect him in a few moments. The pastor pointed out that Jesus was a real human with real emotions who hated the suffering brought on by sin. After the service, Dustin told me privately that God had used my question and his answer to speak to some people in the congregation. The question touched a nerve, and the Spirit prompted them to come forward and pray with the pastor at the altar. This is just one example of God using people to communicate to others. Neither Dustin nor I did anything special. We had no idea what was going on in these people's hearts, but God used us to speak to a hurting family.

Why Bother?

So why bother *listening* to God at all if he's not going to speak? Although I've never heard an audible voice, I can tell you I've had at

---

[18] See Romans 2:12–16.

least (but probably more than) four moments of clarity in my life in which I felt as if God was telling me something specific in the moment when I focused on listening to him.

I'm decent at talking to God: giving him my wish list, asking for forgiveness, and saying thank you. But when it comes to listening, I'm just not that good at it. If you've never spent time in prayer listening to God (rather than just talking), you should give it a shot. Here's how I do it:

I say a quick prayer. I might pray something like, "God please speak to me in this moment if it is your will." This acknowledges that God is in control of the process, not you.

I maintain good posture. I typically sit in a chair, but I don't use the back. In fact, I try not to lean on anything because I tend to fall asleep. You might prefer standing or kneeling.

I (try to) shut off my mind. This is where I falter, but it's an important step. You must silence your inner monologue. You must put your worries to pasture. To help out, I try to picture an image in my mind. For example, I might picture a cross or a beach on the Gulf Coast. Go to your happy place, as they say. Sometimes I focus on a verse I recently read. Sometimes I just focus on breathing. If you're anything like me, you'll lose focus and have to reorient yourself. Don't get discouraged.

I stay still. Be still, trying not to mentally "talk" for a set period of time. How long? A few minutes is enough. I like to set a timer so I don't worry about running late for anything. I can focus on listening without opening my eyes to check the clock.

These are just a few tips that I have discovered along the way. The act of listening might come more naturally to you, but it is definitely difficult for me.

Why It Might Behoove You to Be Quiet

If this all sounds mystical or New-Agey or whatever, it's not. Listening is a critical component of prayer. When we sit still for a few minutes, we are simply opening ourselves up to receive a word from God. This isn't an attempt to control God or trick him into giving you what you want. (Yeah, like that would work anyway.) But how can (and why would) God say anything to you if you don't shut up every now and then? We've all had "conversations" with people who never stop talking. You try to respond or offer your two cents, and they keep talking over you or ignore what you have to say. They aren't interested in dialogue; they just want a sounding board for their monologue.

There are two verses to keep in mind: "Be still, and know that I am God" (Ps. 46:10a) and "When you pray, do not keep on babbling like pagans, for they think they will be heard because of their many words" (Matt. 6:7 NIV). Stillness is okay and babbling is just annoying.

Acts 19 records an incident in Ephesus, a port town on the western coast of modern-day Turkey, in which a silversmith named Demetrius gathered up a mob in protest of the Christian message. Ephesus was famous for its temple honoring the goddess Artemis (called Diana by the Romans). Demetrius complained that Paul had "turned away a great many people, saying that gods made with hands are not gods" (Acts 19:26). Guess what Demetrius did for a living? He made gods with his hands. He was a silversmith who produced idols of Artemis for profit. So he rounded up a bunch of like-minded Ephesians to push back against this new religion of Paul's, which claimed that the god of the Jews, Yahweh, was the one true god, and that Jesus Christ was his incarnation and humanity's only hope for salvation.

With a crowd gathered in the Ephesian theater, Paul attempted to make his way in to give a defense, but his friends barred him from entering for fear he would further incite the crowd and endanger his own life. Instead, the Jewish people in the crowd presented a man named Alexander to make his case for Christ. But when he attempted to speak and the crowd recognized his Jewish heritage, the masses prevented him from speaking by crying out in unison, "Great is Artemis of the Ephesians" (v. 34). They continued chanting in vain repetition for two solid hours!

To paraphrase from Shakespeare's *Hamlet*, the Ephesians doth protest too much, methinks. They held tight to the transmit buttons on their walkie-talkies because they were afraid of what type of response they might get from Alexander—or even worse, they were afraid if they let go of the button and stopped their chant, there would be no response from Artemis at all. I daresay they knew this was the case.

Obviously, Jesus wasn't referring specifically to this incident when he mentioned babbling pagans since it happened after his death, but it seems from Jesus's statement that these types of repetitive, babbling prayers were common among pagans in the first century. But this story is a great example of what Jesus was talking about. Repeating how great Artemis is for two hours is nonsense. And yet pagans must chant and babble because, since their gods are man-made, they will never get a response.

We Christians have no need for babble because we are secure in the transcendent and eternal nature of God. Jesus's point is that God is not real or active or helpful *because* of our prayers, as the pagans believed. Our God is alive and well, and he's active in our lives whether we pray or not. But how do we know our God is the real god and the others are false? I don't have the space here to enumerate the myriad reasons, but for one, Scripture, the oldest surviving and best-preserved text, validates the Judeo-Christian God. Two, our

God is not some machination of human hands or human minds. He is not made of stone or iron or gold, and he wasn't invented by some imaginative people.

John says it another way. He wrote, "In the beginning was the Word, and the Word was with God, and the Word was God" (Jn. 1:1). "Word" here is the Greek *logos*, which means much more than something spoken or written. It means more than the Scriptures. *Logos* speaks to an eternal logic. God is a god of logic and order. As Paul wrote, "God is not a God of confusion but of peace" (1 Cor. 14:33). When you add up all the evidence—creation, morality, Scripture, miracles, the incarnation, and the resurrection—the eternal *logos*, Yahweh, emerges as the one and only true God.

The best proof, though? That just might be hearing from him. And you can't hear from him when you're babbling on like a pagan. No, I've never heard an audible voice, but God has revealed himself and his will to me in ways so clear, you probably wouldn't believe me if I told you. And if I'm wrong? Well, you can go on babbling your prayers. Try listening. You just might hear something.

I'm not claiming that quiet time is always fun and that it won't seem like work sometimes. But isn't this the case for just about anything worthwhile? Take marriage, for example. If you've been married for more than about a week, you know it requires a ton of work, but it can be the most rewarding of human relationships.

There's an old adage posited by speaker Jim Rohn. He said that you become the average of the five people you spend the most time with.[19] I'm not sure how true this is, but the best way I know to become more like Christ is to spend time with him. The more we engage him in prayer and study his Word, the more like Jesus we become.

---

[19] John Rampton, "20 Quotes From Jim Rohn Putting Success and Life Into Perspective," Entrepreneur, Entrepreneur Media Inc., March 4, 2016, https://www.entrepreneur.com/article/271873.

CHAPTER 3

Bursting with Pride

According to Christian teachers, the essential vice, the utmost evil, is Pride. Unchastity, anger, greed, drunkenness, and all that, are mere fleabites in comparison: it was through Pride that the devil became the devil: Pride leads to every other vice: it is the complete anti-God state of mind.
—C. S. Lewis[20]

Two common pitfalls of the Christian life.

I had never heard the term *chuckhole* until I met my wife, Katie. If you also are uninitiated, chuckholes are dents in roads caused by wear or weathering—or, as this Kansan calls them, potholes. The term piqued my curiosity, so I undertook a bit of investigation. Apparently, the term *chuckhole* comes from the effect of running over one of them. One meaning of *chuck* is "an abrupt movement or toss."[21] So when a car or wagon—the term has been around since the early nineteenth century—rolls over a hole in the road, the dent chucks the vehicle. Therefore, people began calling the craters

---

[20] C. S. Lewis, *Mere Christianity* (New York: Macmillan, 1977), 109.

[21] Merriam-Webster, s.v. "chuck," accessed January 16, 2021, https://www.merriam-webster.com/dictionary/chuck.

chuckholes.[22] Perhaps this is mere coincidence and nothing more than anecdotal, but a column in *The Indianapolis Star* claims that although numerous locales have used the term, Indiana newspapers from 1870–2010 used *chuckhole* more often than others.[23] Such a claim resonated with me because, as I said, I'd never encountered the word until I met my wife. And it just so happens that young Katie spent her grade school years in the northeast corner of the Hoosier state.

Not long after Katie and I exchanged our vows, our Ford Taurus tired of functioning. We drove it to a restaurant one frosty December morning and sat down to enjoy a nice breakfast with a friend. The car never drove anywhere again. After having it towed to a mechanic, we got the bad news. The engine was dead. It would cost more to rebuild it than the car was worth. Not great news for a couple of newlywed college students. Nevertheless, we scraped together what little money we had saved, borrowed the rest, and purchased a new fire-engine red Nissan Sentra.

A few months later, Katie was out picking up lunch in the Sentra. Turning into the parking lot of the restaurant, the car suddenly lurched and then stopped. She had driven into one of the largest chuckholes she had ever seen. The hole was so devastating it rendered the car undrivable. We had to call another wrecker to tow the car to a repair shop. In all, the tire and the wheel had to be replaced, and if I remember correctly, the car sustained axle damage too. All from a single pothole.

Whatever you call these depressions in the road, living for God

---

[22] Also written as chuck-hole or chuck hole.

[23] Dawn Mitchell, "Hoosier Lingo: Potholes or Chuckholes?" *The Indianapolis Star*, February 1, 2018, https://www.indystar.com/story/news/history/retroindy/2018/02/01/hoosi er-lingo-potholes-chuckholes/1083894001/.

comes with its own brand of them. Even the most well-intentioned, diligent people fall into these chuckholes at times in their walk with Christ. Thank the Lord for his never-ending grace and mercy. While I think we often give the devil too much credit for our own screwups, he is, no doubt, working his hardest to cause God's people to fall. He is out every day, pickax in hand, hacking away at the straight and narrow. He may not win the war, but he's going to trip up every person he can. Here, we'll look at two of the most common potholes that Christians encounter on their journey to live for God.

When Checking Boxes Is Sexier Than Trusting God

I read somewhere that Ernest Hemingway weighed himself every day, so in an effort to channel his literary genius, I started doing the same. (He also, apparently, recorded the daily result on the wall of his bathroom, but I don't think Katie would appreciate if I tried that.) In the midst of this weird endeavor, I came to a realization. Weight in itself is a meaningless statistic. I could be 175 pounds of pure muscle or 175 pounds of blubber. The number is the same, but one is desirable while the other is unhealthy. If I gain a few pounds, who's to say they aren't muscle? (Other than the proprietor of Kim's Donuts, of course, but I've sworn her to secrecy.) In fact, I'd be rather happy—or at least ambivalent—if I packed on a few pounds of lean body mass. But if those pounds were comprised of fat, then I'd probably be concerned. So you see, weight by itself is largely meaningless; it provides incomplete or misleading data regarding our health. What matters more than mass is body fat percentage.

No doubt I'm telling you something you already know. But if we all know it, why do we still focus so much on weight? It's simple: weight is easy to measure. Body fat percentage? Not so much. Options range from the cheap but inaccurate skin calipers and electrical impedance devices to the expensive or largely inaccessible air pressure chambers, specialized X-ray machines, and underwater weighing tanks (the latter of which, incidentally, do use weight as part of the formula for calculating body composition). At-home body fat scales have become more popular, but engineers are still working to perfect the technology.

So since it is either imprecise or impractical to measure body composition, we continue to stand on the scale morning after morning, using that number as a cheap yardstick of health. If we can get that number down, we hope, we'll be healthier or look a bit better at the beach.

How to Create a Pharisee

The same is true of the Christian life. Just like it's difficult to get an accurate reading of body fat, only God can measure the status of your heart. As God said to the prophet Samuel, "The LORD sees not as man sees: man looks on the outward appearance, but the LORD looks on the heart" (1 Sam. 16:7). And again, as Solomon said in his temple dedication prayer, "You alone know every human heart" (1 Kgs. 8:39 NIV).

There is no button we can press, nothing we can step on, no number we can count to measure our standing with God. Even so, rather than lean on him and trust his diagnosis, we tend to make up our own rubrics so we know how we're doing. We turn towards things we can measure:

How much money we donated.

How many Sundays we made it to church.

How many chapters of the Bible we read.

How many hours we spent in prayer.

How many times we fasted.

How much time we spent volunteering.

All of these things are good, but they are not the measure of a heart close to God. It is quite possible to do all these things—tithe, volunteer, fast, pray, study the Word, and attend church—and still be distant from God. But if you're anything like me, your tendency, however subconscious it might be, is to create checklists of things to do so you can be a *good* Christian. As I check the boxes, I begin to feel good about doing the right things. This in itself is bad enough because we use these artificial rubrics as a way to try to justify ourselves before God when the reality is that justification comes only through faith. Paul wrote as much to the Galatians: "We know that a person is not justified by works of the law but through faith in Jesus Christ" (2:16). Believing God and trusting in his salvation is the only hope we have for *goodness*, i.e. righteousness. Jesus said, "No one is good except God alone" (Lk. 18:19). This includes one who spends every morning in quiet time, donates a tenth of all he has, and volunteers every other weekend. These checkboxes, as sexy as they seem to human eyes, are like the numbers we see when we step on a scale—meaningless in and of themselves.

If these attempts at self-justification are bad, the next progression is even worse. Once someone (or a group of someones) sets up these artificial rubrics, they often begin judging other people by these standards. *The one who doesn't tithe is a heretic. The one who doesn't serve is going to hell.* Maybe it's not so extreme at first, but once the checkboxes are in place, we look down on those who don't tick them. Thus we perpetuate the tradition of the Pharisees. The truth of the matter is that our own righteousness is as filthy as feces, as gross as a bloody discharge.[24]

The problem is that we start with the right intentions (usually),

---

[24] See Isaiah 64:6.

but begin focusing on the symptoms rather than the cause. In reality, I can only do good things because God's Son redeemed me on the cross. I give to the church *because* of all the beautiful things God has given me. I care about people *because* God loves me more than I even know. As C. S. Lewis wrote:

> *The Christian thinks any good he does comes from the Christ-life inside him. He does not think God will love us because we are good, but that God will make us good because He loves us; just as the roof of a greenhouse does not attract the sun because it is bright, but becomes bright because the sun shines on it.*[25]

These good deeds are the effect of a heart right with God, not the cause. But I know I'm guilty of switching the cause and the effect because it seems so much sexier to check a few boxes (and make sure other people know they're checked) than to trust that God will transform my heart from stone to flesh.[26] It seems easier to try to earn my own salvation than to look to the cross and realize that my sins are the nails that bound Jesus to the tree.

Please don't hear me saying that prayer and tithing and the like aren't important; they are. I still step on the scale to see how much I weigh. I just don't put as much stock into that number as I used to. Similarly, don't let external factors be measurements of your spiritual worth. Instead, look to Christ and trust in him. Only he can measure your heart, and only he can make you whole.

---

[25] Lewis, 64.
[26] See Ezekiel 36:26.

What It Really Means to Fear God

If the first chuckhole on the Christian road is the tendency to check off boxes and to take pride in those accomplishments, the second divot in the path comes from a place of pride too. As we establish healthy Christian habits and work to avoid the checkbox mentality pervasive in the church, we will grow closer to God. Yet as we get ever closer to God, we have a tendency to make the same mistake Moses did in the wilderness.

Moses is my favorite Bible character. He was a man of destiny. He was a man of passion. But most importantly, he was seriously close to God. He had actual conversations with the Lord. How awesome (and terrifying) would it be to have audible conversations with God?

From what I can tell, no human was closer to God than Moses was, which is why his fall at Meribah is so tragic and personal to me. If you don't know what I'm talking about, you're not alone. The first time I read it, I had to reread it because the event is subtle. There is no exposition, no explanation. Just God telling Moses that he sinned:

> *"Speak to that rock before their eyes and it will pour out its water." . . . So Moses took the staff from the LORD's presence, just as he commanded him . . . and Moses said to them, "Listen, you rebels, must we bring you water out of this rock?" Then Moses raised his arm and struck the rock twice with his staff. Water gushed out, and the community and their livestock drank. But the LORD said to Moses and Aaron, "Because you did not trust in me enough to honor me as holy in the sight of the Israelites, you will not bring this community into the land I give them."*
> Numbers 20:8–12 (NIV)

When you read the passage carefully, you find that Moses did not follow instructions. God told him to speak to the rock. Instead, he struck it with his staff. But water came out anyway, so what's the big deal? If God didn't approve of his actions, why did he allow the water to flow from the rock?

You must understand all that Moses had been through at this point: rebellion, plagues, committing murder, constant whining from the Israelites, living as a nomad, acting as a judge for Israel, and on and on. He was tired. He was fed up with God's people. He just wanted to rest. So when they arrived at Meribah and the people whined yet again, Moses must have been thinking, *How many times can these people doubt God?* The irony, though, is that in his contempt for God's people and their lack of faith, Moses himself demonstrated a lack of trust by not following God's directions.

But there's another thing in play here. Look again at what Moses said: "Listen, you rebels, must we bring you water out of this rock?" (Num. 20:10). When he used the word "we," he wasn't talking about him and God; he meant him and his brother Aaron. This is the most important issue here. Moses implied that he would provide the people with water; he didn't give God the credit. Moses had become so familiar with God that he failed to give him respect.

Isn't this the struggle all Christians have as they get close to God? We love to hold God up as our *Abba* Father, our Daddy, but in getting so close to him, we sometimes forget that he is also one we should fear—deserving of awe and respect. Don't get me wrong; both of these things are essential to a healthy relationship with God. Look at how Jesus began the Lord's Prayer: "Our Father in heaven, hallowed be your name" (Matt. 6:9). Jesus uses the name *Father*, implying the loving, familial tie we have to our creator, then gives him the respect he deserves by proclaiming his name holy. We like to emphasize the tender, loving side of our relationship with God, sometimes at the expense of the other side. And as Moses found out, as loving as God is, he also commands respect and obedience.

When we probe a bit deeper into this incident, we see that Moses's error was centered on pride. Yes, he was worn out from a dramatic life. Yes, he craved rest in the Promised Land and rest from the Israelites' constant whining. Nevertheless, Moses had grown so close to God that he tried to *play* god. He sought after the same result God wanted—obtaining water from the rock—but he wanted to do it his way and supplant God by taking credit. In reality, Moses was taking advantage of his close relationship with the almighty. He knew God would have his back, so he did the right thing the wrong way. The end result was the same. The Israelites quenched their thirst at Meribah. But the methods did not honor God.

How many times do we do the same thing? I'll use myself as an example. The primary reason I write articles and books is because I believe God has called me to do so. I want to help people. Yes, my desire is to earn a living too. But in the process of writing and publishing, from time to time I receive praise for certain insights or turns of phrase that speak to people. The trick for me is not to let said compliments go to my head, because when I do, I start taking credit for the product rather than giving God the glory. I become prideful rather than acknowledge that God is the very creator and sustainer of life. In essence, I'm taking advantage of my relationship with God by building myself up. I believe this is a serious concern for all who grow close to God—a failure to fear him. Learning to fear God means respecting his will and also refusing to take advantage of our intimate relationship with him for our own glory. We might think we know better than God, but we are wrong.

Jesus Is Our Source of Life

Jesus's temptation in the wilderness stands in contrast to Moses's actions at Meribah.[27] Because Jesus refused to take advantage of his intimate relationship with God and give in to Satan, he fulfilled the purpose his Father laid out for him. After his testing, he ministered for a few years and then died at the hands of murderers so he could serve as an atoning sacrifice for all of humanity. His body was placed in a tomb, and he rose on the third day. After ministering a bit more, he ascended into heaven. This is the essence of the gospel. Where Moses failed, Jesus succeeded. The connection between the two, to me, is no coincidence.

Moses's failure in the desert represents our failures. In pride and anger, Moses struck the rock, water gushed out, and the Israelites drank.[28] Moses's sin and our sins necessitated a Savior, Jesus, to come and take the punishment for our sins. Jesus is our rock who was stricken even though he was innocent so we might have life. On the cross, the culmination of a perfect life, Jesus said, "It is finished" and then died (Jn. 19:30). In a hurry to remove the bodies of Jesus and the two with whom he was crucified due to the impending Jewish holiday, the Jewish leaders asked Pilate to have the legs of these three men broken. Breaking crucified people's legs was the quickest way to usher in death because without the ability to push their bodies up, they could no longer gasp for air and quickly suffocated. But when the Romans came to Jesus and found that he was already dead, they did not break his legs. Nevertheless, to be thorough, a soldier took a spear and pierced Jesus's side. As a result, blood and water came rushing out.

Earlier in his ministry, Jesus said, "Whoever drinks of the water

---

[27] More on this in chapter nine.
[28] Numbers 20:11.

that I will give him will never be thirsty again. The water that I will give him will become in him a spring of water welling up to eternal life" (Jn. 4:14). So you see, where Moses failed, Jesus did not. Jesus is the rock stricken for us to cover our sins of pride and hypocrisy. While Moses claimed to bring the water out of the rock on his own, only Jesus can give us water that leads to eternal life.

CHAPTER 4

The Counterintuitive Way to Elevate Your Faith

We simply cannot do anything alone. Any growth or progress in the spiritual life cannot be traced to our paltry efforts. All is the work of grace.

—Brennan Manning[29]

Admitting we need God is a game changer.

If someone were to ask you how best to increase your faith, you might conjure up a lengthy list of to-dos to beef up your spiritual muscles. These are things we've already discussed in previous chapters: studying the Word, serving the poor, praying, fasting, giving money to the church and to charity. All of these answers, while good, share a common bond. Serving and giving and the like all center around actions we take. Again, these are positive, important symptoms of a healthy Christian walk. Just as James wrote, "As the body apart from the spirit is dead, so also faith apart from works is dead" (2:26). Our faith informs and fuels our actions. If we say we

---

[29] Brennan Manning, *The Relentless Tenderness of Jesus* (Grand Rapids, MI: Revell, 2011), Kindle edition, 65.

believe God and his Word and yet do not heed it, of what value is our belief?

And yet, there's another way to elevate your faith that is much less glamorous than serving soup for the homeless. It is more difficult and seems to run counter to common sense. I'm talking about relying on God.

In my third year of high school, we juniors spent some time studying the romantic writers of nineteenth-century America. I found myself captivated by the ideals proposed by the likes of Ralph Waldo Emerson, who espoused self-reliance and personal freedom. Then, in my first year of college, I dove even deeper into the transcendentalist writers in my American Literature class. Perhaps it's my introversion or my Americanness, but these ideas resonated with me. For a time, I became fascinated with the transcendentalist movement, latching on to such platitudes as "No kernel of nourishing corn can come to him but through his toil bestowed on that plot of ground which is given to him to till."[30] What an attractive proposition for the rugged individualist. We may eat, suggests Emerson, but we can only be nourished when we supply ourselves with the food. There lies within this statement, no doubt, an element of truth. How much more satisfying is a dollar earned through sweat and strain than the dollar given by a parent, or worse—by the government? King Solomon's wisdom can speak to this truth. He wrote, "There is nothing better for a person than that he should eat and drink and find enjoyment in his toil. This also, I saw, is from the hand of God" (Eccl. 2:24). And yet, as tempted as I am to wager all of my philosophical capital and go all in on this idea of self-reliance, Emerson's metaphor slyly leaves out one important element of raising corn. Without rain and sunlight, we could never produce even a

---

[30] Ralph Waldo Emerson, "Self-Reliance," in *The Norton Anthology of American Literature: Shorter Fifth Edition*, ed. Nina Baym (New York: W. W. Norton and Company, 1991), 551.

single kernel. We may till the soil, plant the seeds in neat little rows, and fertilize the ground, but without water and solar energy, nothing would grow. Emerson takes for granted the grace and provision of God almighty.

The Scriptures remind us that "God is light, and in him is no darkness at all" (1 Jn. 1:5) and that he is "the fountain of living waters" (Jer. 2:13). And Jesus, the second person of the Trinity, holds all life together.[31] We take these natural realities for granted, as if sunlight and rainfall are automatic because the sun rose yesterday and it rained last week. But what if the earth spinning on its axis was more will than necessity? The English apologist G. K. Chesterton suggested as much. He wrote, "It is possible that God says every morning, 'Do it again' to the sun; and every evening, 'Do it again' to the moon.... The repetition in Nature may not be a mere recurrence; it may be a theatrical *encore*.... Repetition may go on for millions of years, by mere choice, and at any instant it may stop."[32] God is the source of all life, so to assume we could raise even a single nourishing kernel on our own would be to presume upon the Creator.

Now, you might be thinking it's obvious that we should rely on God. Who would disagree with such a proposition? But although every Christian would assent to this idea, how many of us actually live it out? How often do we try to control everything in our lives? How often do we fail to consult God for our big and small decisions? And how often do we miss out on opportunities to further the kingdom because of fear? These are all symptoms of a life not really relying on God. I know I'm often guilty of failing to depend on God, and I have to refocus on him and not my problems or my plans. King

---

[31] Colossians 1:17.

[32] G. K. Chesterton, *Orthodoxy* (Chicago: Moody Classics, 2009), Kindle edition, 92.

Solomon wrote, "In their hearts humans plan their course, but the LORD establishes their steps" (Prov. 16:9 NIV). We often think we know the best course for our lives, but many times God has better plans. This isn't only true in the big things but also in the day-to-day doings of our lives, and it starts with our natural weaknesses.

The Great Thing about Weaknesses

I may not know you, but I know something about you. God created you with certain strengths. Yes, nurture plays an important role, but these strengths are embedded in your DNA, often emerging even when you are young.

But if we are all born with strengths, a necessary corollary is that we all possess certain weaknesses. He who excels at mathematics might struggle with prose. She who is gracious might struggle with self-esteem. Nevertheless, weaknesses, despite evidence to the contrary, are good things. Weaknesses provide us with opportunities to rely on God and on others in areas where we struggle. Take empathy, for example. I'm not great at empathizing with others. I wish it came more naturally, but it's simply not one of my strengths. For my wife, Katie, on the other hand, this is probably her greatest strength. But although empathy is a great thing, it's actually good that I'm not good at it. In deferring to Katie, I'm learning to look outside myself to help me understand what others are feeling.

God created you with some strengths and with some weaknesses. You can't be good at everything. Otherwise you'd be God. And no matter how hard you work on your weaknesses, they'll never become strengths. You might get incrementally better at them, but they won't come naturally. Seems kind of counterintuitive, right? The way to become more excellent is by admitting we are less excellent. But Scripture backs this up. Paul wrote to the Corinthians that the Lord told him, "My grace is sufficient for you, for my power is made perfect in weakness" (2 Cor. 12:9). The interesting thing here is that the word weakness comes from the Greek *astheneia*, which can also be translated as *infirmity*. In fact, Paul uses the same word in the following sentence, and the King James Version uses "infirmity" in this second instance: "Most gladly therefore will I rather glory in my infirmities, that the power of Christ may rest upon me."

Therefore, we should not limit our definition of weaknesses just to a lack of skills or abilities in a certain realm; we should include physical limitations as well. Paul, in 2 Corinthians, writes about a certain thorn in his flesh. Conjecture and debate abound regarding said "thorn," which includes some commentators who claim the thorn was not a physical one. I won't enter into that fray because I have no special knowledge or insight into Paul's thorn, and because it really doesn't matter much for our discussion here whether the infirmity was physical or psychological. Either way, Paul's weakness was ultimately for God's glory, and even for his own benefit. As he wrote, "For when I am weak, then I am strong" (12:10).

So what's the takeaway for those of us who may not have a messenger of Satan harassing us? Weaknesses can come in many forms, like cancer, a bad knee, or a high-strung Achilles tendon. If God's behind some of these infirmities, doesn't that make him out to be a big jerk? Absolutely not. Remember, he knows what's best for us. As Jesus said, "What does it profit a man to gain the whole world and forfeit his soul?" (Mk. 8:36). God concerns himself much more with your eternal status than with the here and now. If it means a broken bone to humble someone to seek out his grace, isn't it worth it?

Nevertheless, we should not be so quick to ascribe pain and suffering to our maker. I think people are too hasty in giving God credit for earthly maladies. When HIV exploded among the gay community in the 1980s, some evangelicals were quick to announce the virus was God's retribution on homosexuality.[33] Similarly, a handful of prominent clergy deemed the terrorist attacks in New York and on the Pentagon on September 11, 2001 as punishment for America turning away from God.[34] My question is, how do they know? Paul knew because God told him so. Are we to believe these people heard the voice of God?

We must, then, make a distinction between what God causes and what God allows to happen. Let's take an easy one as an example: September 11, 2001. Could God have violated the free will of the terrorists and caused them to hijack jets and fly them into the World Trade Center, the Pentagon, and a field in Western Pennsylvania as punishment for the ever-increasing apostasy of the United States of America? Of course he *could*. He's God. But isn't it so much more likely that evil men, deluded and given to dishonorable passions, carried out the attacks of their own volition? If such is the case, God merely allowed the evil to occur rather than having caused it. What's the difference, you might ask? Since he was able to stop it, isn't he still in the wrong?

No. I won't belabor the point since I've written about this elsewhere, but such a stance fails to account for two things: time and God's omnipotence. God allows suffering to persist for a short time so as many people as possible turn to him. As 2 Peter 3:9 tells us,

---

[33] See, for example, Jerry Falwell, who said, "AIDS is not just God's punishment for homosexuals, it is God's punishment for the society that tolerates homosexuals." As quoted in Matt Stearns, "Jerry Falwell: 1933–2007," *Daily Press*, May 16, 2007, https://www.dailypress.com/news/dp-xpm-20070516-2007-05-16-0705160055-story.html.

[34] Robert Jeffress suggested as much at his Liberty University convocation speech in 2015. See Liberty University, "Dr. Robert Jeffress—Liberty University Convocation," YouTube video, 38:34, March 31, 2015, https://youtu.be/23SFznWrUao?t=819.

"The Lord is not slow to fulfill his promise as some count slowness, but is patient toward you, not wishing that any should perish, but that all should reach repentance." While suffering in the moment feels like a long time, in the light of eternity it's but a vapor. In addition, God's omnipotence affords him the power to restore what is lost, whether on this side of eternity or the other.

All of this brings us back to God's grace. The truth is that whether or not God is the direct source of infirmities, disabilities, and weaknesses, he can use them for good. That's how God works. God offers as much grace as we need and more. I will be the first to admit my life has seen but a drop of pain and suffering compared to the oceans others have had to endure. But I also know that God is faithful and will assist you through whatever hardship you endure. How do I know? Because God said as much to Paul: "My grace is sufficient for you" (2 Cor. 12:9a). When we learn to rely on God, we boost our faith to levels higher than we could imagine. As Paul put it, "When I am weak, then I am strong" (v. 10).

A Declaration of Interdependence

When I broke my right foot, I could not envision all the negative ramifications that the fracture would bring with it. In fact, I didn't even know my foot was broken at all. But I did know that ankles aren't supposed to swell to the size of a softball, and I also knew such a magnitude of pain was abnormal for a typical trampoline accident. Which brings me to the first consequence of foot-breaking: if you're going to break your foot, make sure you have a great story behind the break, because everyone who sees you in a cast, boot, crutches, or one of those sissy knee scooters is going to ask. I was tempted to make up some epic story involving BASE jumping, monster trucks, or saving a baby from a fire (or all three!), but inevitably I stuck to some version of the following.

After picking my kids up from school on their last day before Christmas break, we spent some quality time on the trampoline, during which I experienced my own type of break. My four kids and I piled into the mesh cage, violating just about every safety rule found on the faded and half-torn warning label. My youngest child, Abe, was three and a half at the time, so he liked to be picked up while we jumped so we he wouldn't fall down as often. I liked to pick him up while we jumped so he was less likely to get killed by my wild-child oldest son, Thomas, who was twelve at the time.

One tradition I'm particularly proud of passing down to Thomas is The Double Bounce (trademark pending), sometimes also referred to as The Boost (trademark pending). If you've spent any amount of time on a trampoline, you've likely discovered The Double Bounce yourself (even if only by accident), but here's how it goes. You and another person time your jumps so that one lands just prior to the other. As the second person is landing, the trampoline is on its way back up from the first person's jump, snapping the second jumper back up into the air much higher than he could have jumped on his own.

I'm not sure if anyone loves The Double Bounce more than Thomas, both as recipient and giver. On this particular December day—December 17, to be exact—Thomas decided to give me the best boost of my life. Truth be told, the bounce would have been of epic proportions had my ankle held up under the strain. The problem is that I was holding sweet Abe in my left arm when Thomas surreptitiously approached from my right side to initiate The Double Bounce. Bearing Abe's extra forty pounds added additional torque to the snap of the trampoline's canvas, and my foot was caught in the middle.

Upon landing, my ankle rolled, shifting all of the momentum and force to my foot, whereupon my fifth metatarsal also cried "uncle" as it cracked under the pressure. Eyewitnesses claim I shouted "Mother!" when the break occurred, a claim this author vehemently denies. All I remember from that moment is an intense shooting pain originating from my foot. The experience was one of those out-of-body things for a brief instant, because I recall shouting in pain before I actually felt any. I remember wondering why I was shouting and then a millisecond later thinking, "Oh that's why." In a move that only boosted my already strong Father-of-the-Year credentials, I managed to return Abe to the mat as I fell rather than chuck the toddler, as just about everything inside of me wanted to do.

I could fill pages with the bizarre and comical details of my accident, but I will abstain primarily because the more I embellish, the more I fear I'll sound like a wimp. So I'll wrap up with a few details. Adrenaline is my only theory for how I made my way back inside the house. Once inside, I had the foresight to take some NSAIDs and ice my ankle, which did swell to about the size of a healthy grapefruit. In retrospect, it was obvious my foot was broken. As I replay the incident in my mind, I can feel the bone cracking under the torque of the mat. It hurts just thinking about it. And after about thirty minutes, the pain had gone from "ouch" to "just shoot me."

My wife, Katie, conveniently enough, is a Registered Nurse. But that fact is only convenient when she's not on hour ten of a twelve-hour shift at the hospital. I crawled under the love seat in our living room to protect the foot from little children who love to jump on their dad and don't understand what broken bones are and why they shouldn't be jumped on.

My text messages were nonchalant at first. "Any way you could get off early?" I didn't want to alarm Katie in case an early departure from her shift was not a possibility. But she knew, as she always does, that something was up. The hospital is only a few miles from our house, so I postulate she must have heard my scream the moment the fracture occurred.

"Why? What's up?!"

"I hurt my ankle."

If she didn't leave early, I'd have had to hole up in my couch cave for another two hours while the littles pillow-fought to the death.

Katie made it home about thirty minutes later, helped me limp into our SUV, and then headed right back to her workplace to drop me off at the ER. She parked the car at the entrance with kids in tow, retrieved a wheelchair from inside, wheeled me in, and took the kids back home. I waited over an hour to be seen, after which an X-ray confirmed the break. They fit me with a soft cast to stabilize the extremity, prescribed me some pills, and advised me to call an orthopedic doctor.

It's probably for the best that I couldn't have foreseen all the complications of the injury, or else my spirits would have dipped way sooner than they did. The worst part was not the trauma or even the multi-hour ER wait. No, the hardest part for me was the inability to be self-sufficient. I suffered a pseudo-Jones fracture on the fifth metatarsal—a fancy way to say I broke my pinky toe bone about halfway up my foot. As traumatic injuries go, this is probably the least bad one I could imagine. And like I said, I could deal with the pain, but it was the lameness that had me down.

Since the injury happened so close to Christmas, I had to wait a full week after my ER visit before seeing a doctor. During that week I was an invalid, lying on the couch like a bum. But my spirits were still high, and I started hopping on my left foot to get around. Probably not the greatest plan. Toward the end of the week, I was hopping to the kitchen to prepare dinner when I felt a sharp pain in my foot—my good foot. Since my right foot was useless, my left was bearing all the weight, and it had finally reached its limit. I limped back to the couch and started to despair. I went from two good feet to zero in a matter of a few days.

When I finally got in to see the doc, he fitted me with a boot and prescribed eight weeks in it. Eight weeks. Remember, this was my right foot, so I could not drive (believe me, I tried—I don't recommend it). I had to have Katie or her mom take me everywhere. I had to have help with doors. I had to have help getting into the shower.

As Christians, let's assume the obvious. We can't produce even a single nourishing grain of corn without God's provision—the rain and the sunshine. With that foundation of God's provision in place, we can then become self-reliant, right?

As romantic as that notion is to a rugged individualist and introvert like myself, Emerson's self-reliance is an illusion. Even if we assume God will be faithful because he always has been, God still calls us to community. We are dependent on God for life itself, but can one ever be independent? For a time, perhaps, but what my physical limitation taught me is that as fallen, imperfect beings with inherent weakness, we would all do well to learn interdependence. This is the idea of a mutual state of dependence in which people rely on each other to assist in their limitations.

As much I love the idea of self-reliance, of putting Ralph Emerson on a pedestal, interdependence is biblical: "There are different kinds of gifts, but the same Spirit distributes them . . . to each one the manifestation of the Spirit is given for the common good" (1 Cor. 12:4, 7 NIV). Did you catch that last part? The Spirit gives us gifts in order to promote the common good. Not only do we need to learn to accept help from others in our limitations, but we should also use our own gifts and strengths to help others out. When the body of Christ comes together, complementing each other with our strengths, we become the best possible vessel for the gospel.

As an introvert, I must admit this is very difficult for me. I like to take care of my own business. I dislike relying on other people. I hate asking for help. But breaking my foot forced me to admit my limitations and accept help from other people. I'm still not great at interdependence, but I'm learning as I go along that God desires for us to be a community of believers, complementing each other's strengths and covering each other's weaknesses. When we do this, we become the best church possible—more loving, more effective, and more attractive to the lost. My hope is that you need not suffer trauma to learn this valuable lesson.

Don't worry about your weaknesses. Use your strengths to honor God and rely on him for the rest.

This Simple Mindset Shift Will Revolutionize Your Life

This is all well and good. Maybe you're on board with dependence on God. Even still, the question remains: how do we rely on God? What does that look like in the Christian's life? Before answering that question, let's examine a more mundane one. *Why are there so many weight loss programs and books?*

The short answer, probably, is that they sell. As long as the demand exists, people will continue to produce these products en masse. But I think there's a deeper answer. I think weight loss programs abound because no two people are exactly alike. Whether it's keto, intermittent fasting, South Beach, Atkins, Weight Watchers, Jenny Craig, P90X, Crossfit, Prancercise, you name it, every human body is unique and responds to different diet and exercise plans differently. Therefore, what works for one person may not work for the next. For every weight loss success story one could create a new, unique plan.

In the same way, I don't think there exists some universal

prescriptive plan for how one learns to rely on God and live it out day by day. Again, we are all unique with unique strengths and weaknesses, and that uniqueness is multiplied exponentially when combined with our own individual contexts. It's not nature *plus* nurture; it's nature *times* nurture.

Nevertheless, as with weight loss—burn more calories than you consume—we can find some small degree of universality that will be useful across the board to believers. I think one component of that universality resides in our mindset. In the first part of this chapter, we discussed learning to own our weaknesses and admit we need God to fill those gaps with his grace and mercy. The way we elevate our faith, then, is not by adding another item to our task list but rather by living our lives expecting that God will provide that grace and mercy. What does this look like? Again, this is hard to prescribe because it looks so different for each person, but some examples might help:

When you're considering a job change, do you seek God's guidance?

When your day doesn't go as planned, do you respond with anger or do you look for ways to honor God?

When illness strikes, do you lean on God for grace to endure?

Now, I know what you might be thinking: prayer *is* doing something. That is true, but it is actually a symptom of a life that relies on God. We turn to him in expectation that he'll provide our next job, that he'll heal our bodies, that he'll tell the sun to "do it again" tomorrow. We pray not to get stuff or to check a box on our list, but as people acknowledging our need for his provision. Just as Jesus taught us to pray when he said, "Give us this day our daily bread" (Matt. 6:11), we acknowledge we cannot provide anything of our own accord.

But prayer isn't the only avenue for living a life of expectation.

When we go to church, do we enter the sanctuary expecting God to show up and do something amazing? When tragedy strikes, do we anticipate his provision, grace, and healing? Even when I sit down to write a new chapter or article, most days I think, *I can't do this*. And I'm right.

Are you pessimistic or optimistic? Which attitude do you think better reflects a life lived in expectation of God's provision? I'll be honest—sometimes it takes a large amount of faith to be optimistic when we look at what's going on in our world, doesn't it?

What you say, how you pray, how you plan for the future, even your body language all reflect whether or not you expect God to show up. But once you commit to this expectation mindset, you'll see your faith grow exponentially. Living in anticipation of God's provision is a critical step in elevating your faith, but there is one trap to avoid as you progress down this path.

You Deserve a Sopapilla

After the sheer glut of food that arrives via the eager wait staff at the modern Oklahoma Mexican restaurant comes the sopapillas.

If you're uninitiated, sopapillas are little pillows of deep-fried flour, cinnamon, and sugar, and tradition dictates you douse them with honey before consuming them. Tradition also tells us that these delectables are pro bono, a courtesy for overcoming the vast amounts of chips, cheese, and beans placed before the diner. The server need only say one word—"Sopapillas?"—and the regular knows what's about to go down. Within minutes, small plates topped with the warm, deep-fried dessert are set before customers who, just a short time prior, couldn't possibly eat another bite.

So you can imagine my ire when, one day, Katie and I finished our tacos and, rather than the sopapillas, the check came instead. As it turned out, this particular Mexican cafe broke ranks and stopped offering the dessert for free. *But we always receive sopapillas*, I thought. *We deserve them!* We ate our way through the meal; we did our part. Now come the sopapillas.

But they never came. (Woe was I.)

If I come off sounding like a spoiled brat, well, you're right. I am one.

Yet in the same manner, those who learn to live in expectation of God's provision and grace can fall into a similar trap. If they are not careful, they can begin to take grace for granted. They begin to believe they deserve God's provision. Remember our example of Moses from chapter three? Moses was so in step with God that he knew the Lord would provide water for the Israelites. So Moses grew cocky, failing to offer the fear and gratitude God deserves.

We should not live with expectation because we feel entitled or in some way deserving, but rather because God is faithful. When Jesus offered to go and heal the centurion's servant, the centurion said something that impressed Jesus. He said, "Lord, I am not worthy to have you come under my roof, but only say the word, and my servant will be healed" (Matt. 8:8). Do remember how Jesus responded?

> *When Jesus heard this, he marveled and said to those who followed him, "Truly, I tell you, with no one in Israel have I found such faith. I tell you, many will come from east and west and recline at table with Abraham, Isaac, and Jacob in the kingdom of heaven, while the sons of the kingdom will be thrown into the outer darkness. In that place there will be weeping and gnashing of teeth."* Matthew 8:10–12

Why was Jesus astounded? What point was he getting at? God chose the people of Israel to be his own. They had a special, covenantal relationship with Yahweh. And as a result, many veered off into a sense of entitlement. What need have you for faith if you believe you deserve God's hand of provision and grace? In fact, grace, by definition, is unmerited, so not a single human being can ever deserve it. Real faith, then, is knowing you are sinful and undeserving and yet believing that God will still give us the grace that he promises us.

Contrast this attitude with the Pharisees of the day, who lived with a sense of entitlement simply because they descended from Abraham. They must have forgotten the words Moses spoke to the Israelites:

> *It was not because you were more in number than any other people that the LORD set his love on you and chose you, for you were the fewest of all peoples, but it is because the LORD loves you and is keeping the oath that he swore to your fathers.*
> Deuteronomy 7:7–8

Translation: they didn't deserve God either.

Sometimes we churchgoers are guilty of possessing this same sense of entitlement rather than exhibiting the humility of the centurion. Just like I felt entitled to sopapillas, we go to church every Sunday taking for granted that the Holy Spirit will show up. Truth is, we don't deserve for Jesus to come under our church roof any more than the centurion did. Even though we may be saved and cleansed of our sins, atonement comes by grace, not by merit.

So this simple mindset shift will absolutely revolutionize your life: approach every day expecting the God to show up—not because we deserve it, but with a confident yet humble faith like the centurion demonstrated.

Part II

From Prosperity to Disillusionment: When Excellence Isn't Enough

CHAPTER 5

How to Receive God's Blessings (You Greedy Heel Grabber)

Wealth is uncertain—but God's provision is constant.
—Dave Ramsey[35]

Lessons on abundance from David, Solomon, and Jacob.

So you want to receive God's blessings? Welcome to the club.

As you commit to strengthening your spiritual life and growing in your faith, it often follows that good things come your way. Growing closer to God, in fact, is its own reward, an intrinsic blessing. But how can we receive other blessings in our lives? What does the Bible have to say about receiving God's provision and favor? The first place we'll turn is the book of Psalms. If there was anyone in the Bible who knew about divine blessing, it was David. His name means "beloved," and God chose him as the king of Israel and forefather of Jesus. So when David wrote about blessing, he probably knew what he was talking about. Here's an excerpt from the

---

[35] Dave Ramsey, *The Legacy Journey: A Radical View of Biblical Wealth and Generosity* (Brentwood, TN: Ramsey Press, 2014), Kindle edition, location 521 of 2961.

Twenty-Fourth Psalm, in which David wrote about blessing:

> *Who shall ascend the hill of the LORD?*
> *And who shall stand in his holy place?*
> *He who has clean hands and a pure heart,*
> *who does not lift up his soul to what is false*
> *and does not swear deceitfully.*
> *He will receive blessing from the LORD*
> *and righteousness from the God of his salvation.*
> *Such is the generation of those who seek him,*
> *who seek the face of the God of Jacob.*
> Psalm 24:3–6

Three things stand out to me in this passage. (We'll get to the third point later on). The first is that those who receive God's blessings are of the generation of those who seek God. No need to belabor this point, since we addressed in some detail what it looks like to seek after God in the first part of this book. Second is that a necessary component of seeking God is integrity—or, as the psalmist wrote, "clean hands and a pure heart" (Ps. 24:4). Such a person, David tells us, will receive blessings from the Lord.

The hands are a metaphor for our actions, since by them we conduct our work. Therefore, to have clean hands means to be guiltless in our conduct. If that wasn't difficult enough, the psalm doesn't stop there. We must also possess pure hearts. The heart, of course, represents our motivation and intent. In other words, one must conduct his or her life with virtue not only in deed but on the inside as well.

As you know, it is quite possible, at least for a time, to do and say the right things while on the inside your mind is debased and full of sin. David, though, underscores the importance of possessing a "pure heart." This is integrity: doing the right and honest thing—regardless of whether anyone is watching and regardless of the consequences—because it is the right thing to do. Those who live with integrity adhere to a moral code that exists outside of themselves. For the Christian, this code is God's moral law. The psalmist, then, reminds us that not only are our actions important but so are our motivations. Or, to state it more plainly, it's not okay to do the right thing for the wrong reason.

During his ministry, Jesus reserved some of his harshest words for those who did the right things with the wrong motivations. In his Sermon on the Mount, Jesus said, "When you give to the needy, sound no trumpet before you, as the hypocrites do in the synagogues and in the streets, that they may be praised by others" (Matt. 6:2). Giving to the needy? Good. Doing so to receive praise from others? Not so good. As Jesus said later in his ministry about the Pharisees and scribes, "They do all their deeds to be seen by others" (Matt. 23:5).

This isn't the only reason people do the right things for the wrong reasons, but it's a biggie. We're wired to be part of a community, and who doesn't like to be liked? There's nothing wrong with being well liked, and people who live with integrity are often held in high esteem. But Jesus taught that our motivation for good deeds should be to please God. Rather than announce your generous gifts to the poor, Jesus said you should "not let your left hand know what your right hand is doing, so that your giving may be in secret. And your Father who sees in secret will reward you" (Matt 6:3–4). Even still, we don't give in secret so that we will be rewarded by God, but instead we give in secret to honor and please God, and as a result, he rewards us. This is a subtle but important point. Those who receive God's blessings live with integrity because it is the right thing to do.

The Proverbial Blueprint

David gives us an excellent description of one who receives God's blessings, but we would be remiss to stop there. The book of Proverbs is chock-full of wisdom and advice regarding prosperity, and David's son Solomon receives credit for writing the majority of the book. Not only was Solomon rich but he was also the wisest man who ever lived. As a result, he had quite a few things to say about blessings from God. Although he enumerates other characteristics, Solomon's blueprint for blessing boils down to three main actions.

The first step is one we just discussed above: those who would receive good things from God live their lives with integrity. Read, for example, Proverbs 10:6, which teaches that "blessings are on the head of the righteous," or Proverbs 28:20, which says that "A faithful man will abound with blessings." Or perhaps read that "The LORD's curse is on the house of the wicked, but he blesses the dwelling of the righteous" (Prov. 3:33). These Proverbs echo David's assertion that those who are upright will receive blessings.

The second requirement is hard work. How many people do you know who expect to become rich without working hard? They see celebrities on television or business moguls in the news and desire to be just like those people without realizing how hard those people worked to become the best in their industries. Full disclosure, I had similar delusions regarding my authorial pursuits, believing money would flow my way simply because I'm special. In reality, I *am* special, and so are you—just like everyone else.

So what does Proverbs have to say about hard work? Chapter 10, verse 4 tells us, "A slack hand causes poverty, but the hand of the diligent makes rich." Proverbs 13:4 teaches that "the soul of the sluggard craves and gets nothing, while the soul of the diligent is richly supplied." And once more, "The plans of the diligent lead surely to abundance" (Prov. 21:5). These verses contrast the behavior of the lazy with that of the diligent. With laziness comes a tendency to embrace the get-rich-quick attitude. Proverbs, though, emphasizes hard, careful, and conscientious work over a prolonged period of time. Not as sexy as winning the lottery, is it?

The last requirement is the importance of seeking wisdom. Doing so involves increasing knowledge, leaning on wise people, and being humble enough to know you need wisdom. Proverbs uses the word "fool" or some form thereof seventy-one times in the English Standard Version. Solomon is trying to warn his readers against foolishness and steer them toward wisdom. And if there is any subject on which Solomon was an authority, it is this right here. Shortly after he became king of Israel, the Lord appeared to him in a dream and told him to ask for anything he wanted. Where do our minds wander when we imagine such a proposition? I'd venture to say that many people would seek either pleasure or security. Both of these things can be obtained with money. A million dollars can buy a lot of fun, and it can provide some superficial level of security. Others might ask for good health or revenge against their enemies. They might try to secure the welfare of their loved ones. They might ask for someone who would love them. Solomon asked for none of these things. Instead, he asked God for a discerning mind. In response, God said:

> Because you have asked this, and have not asked for yourself long life or riches or the life of your enemies, but have asked for yourself understanding to discern what is right, behold, I now do according to your word. Behold, I give you a wise and discerning mind, so that none like you has been before you and none like you shall arise after you. I give you also what you have not asked, both riches and honor, so that no other king shall compare with you, all your days.
> 1 Kings 3:11–13

Do you see what happened here? Solomon asked for wisdom, and as a result, God blessed him. In essence, the blessings were a byproduct of wisdom. As the passage says, Solomon is the wisest man who ever lived, so when he writes about wisdom, we would do well to listen. Who is wise? Those who fear the Lord, seek knowledge, and accept instruction.[36] Those who are slow to anger and slow to speak, and who, when they do talk, speak truth.[37]

So to sum up Solomon's advice for receiving God's blessings, we must live honest lives (have integrity), work with diligence, and seek out wisdom. Easy as pie, right? But there's actually one more thing the book of Proverbs advises for those who would receive the blessings of God. I saved it for last because it merits a lengthier discussion.

How to Burst Your Vats

The last proverbial key for unlocking God's blessings is generosity. For some, it may seem obvious that generosity is a prerequisite for blessing, while for others such an idea may seem counterintuitive. We receive by giving things away? Regardless of your stance, the book of Proverbs doesn't lack clarity on the issue. Chapter eleven teaches, "One gives freely, yet grows all the richer; another withholds what he should give, and only suffers want" (v. 24). Proverbs 3:9–10 reads, "Honor the LORD with your wealth and with the firstfruits of all your produce; then your barns will be filled with plenty, and your vats will be bursting with wine." Generosity isn't really optional, and the opposite mindset leads to destitution: "A stingy man hastens after wealth and does not know that poverty will come upon him" (Prov. 28:22).

---

[36] See Proverbs 1:7, 15:2, et al.
[37] See Proverbs 10:10, 10:18, 14:29, et al.

Some people get this concept backwards. They think, "Once God blesses me, then I'll start giving." The Proverbs, though, show that we are to give freely and should not be stingy. And, in doing so, we honor our creator, who is the best example of generosity. He pours out blessings on his people and offered his own Son for our sakes so that we might receive the ultimate gift: grace via the shed blood of Christ. As Christians, we manifest generosity in many ways, which includes extending forgiveness to others as we have received forgiveness. We should also be generous with time and other resources. And we can't escape the subject of generosity without talking about everyone's favorite subject: money, specifically charitable giving. For the Christian, the foundation of charity is the tithe.

Now I know what you might be thinking: "Does the command to tithe *really* apply to Christians?" If you are having such doubts, you're not alone. In 2017, Lifeway surveyed American churchgoers about tithing. The majority (83%) of respondents agreed that the tithe is a Biblical command that still applies today. And yet, only 54% of those surveyed said that they give at least a tenth of their income to their church.[38]

Everyone struggles with his or her own issues, and no doubt one of those issues centers around money in the same way that others struggle with lust or anger or alcohol. After all, as Paul reminds us, "The love of money is a root of all kinds of evils" (1 Tim. 6:10). But I think there's another wrinkle here to account for the disparity between money and mouth, so to speak. Maybe a good amount of those 29% of people who say tithing is a current Biblical mandate

---

[38] *Churchgoer Views—Tithing: Representative Survey of 1010 American Churchgoers*, August 30, 2017, distributed by LifeWay Research, http://lifewayresearch.com/wp-content/uploads/2018/05/American-Churchgoers-Tithing-2017.pdf, slides 5 and 7.

but don't tithe don't actually believe it. They might say they do, and might even think they believe it, but their actions tell a different story. So the question we need to clear up is this: is tithing a New Covenant mandate, or is it just some liturgical hoax that pastors employ to ensure revenue? Before answering that question, though, we should establish some important truths.

First, God doesn't need your money. Anyone who holds to this line of thinking is fooling himself. God created the universe; he created all matter. To think he needs our dollars would be a bit like assuming the creator of Super Mario needs Mario to bring him coins. Even if he did need coins, he could simply reprogram the game to his desire. The assertion that God needs our money to achieve his will is ludicrous. Can he use our gifts to accomplish his purposes? Absolutely. But he can also speak life into existence, raise people from the dead, and part the seas.

Second, while the word "tithe" literally means *tenth*, because it appears that God commanded multiple tithes, the total percentage given might have been closer to 20%. For example, if I give a tithe of $100 dollars to the Levites, I'd have $90 left. If I were then to tithe on the remainder for use in worship to God, I'd have $81 left.[39] This example is an oversimplification, but you get the point.

Should Christians Tithe?

Now to the matter at hand. Is the tithe a mandate that applies to New Covenant believers? Proponents of this view will point to Matthew 23 (and its corresponding passage in Luke 11) in which Jesus rebuked the Pharisees for their illogical approach to the Law. He said, "Woe to you, scribes and Pharisees, hypocrites! For you tithe

---

[39] See Numbers 18 and Deuteronomy 14 for more details.

mint and dill and cumin, and have neglected the weightier matters of the law: justice and mercy and faithfulness. *These you ought to have done*, without neglecting the others" (v. 23, emphasis mine).

Jesus didn't say tithing is unimportant; he said they ought to have done so, just not at the expense of the more critical components of the Law. Nevertheless, to claim this "ought to" applies to New Covenant believers might be a stretch. Jesus's audience was made up of teachers of the Law and other religious leaders, those bound to the Mosaic covenant. To assume this statement is prescriptive to those not bound to the Law of Moses is probably a mistake.

But don't think we're off the hook just yet. A couple of New Testament passages speak to the idea of giving. The first is when some Jews tested Jesus about paying taxes to Rome. They were trying to trick Jesus into teaching against remitting tax so that they could report him to the Roman authorities. Instead, Jesus asked for a coin. He asked, "'Whose likeness and inscription is this?' They said, 'Caesar's.' Then he said to them, 'Therefore render to Caesar the things that are Caesar's, and to God the things that are God's'" (Matt. 22:20–21). So Jesus taught we should give to God that which belongs to him. Do you realize the implications of this statement? God owns everything. He doesn't just want a tenth; he wants your all. Am I saying Christians should give 100% of their income to the church? No, probably not, unless the Spirit directs you to do so. This is more of a heart issue than one of finances. But if we can't muster 10% of our income, are our hearts really in line with God? I can't answer that for you, since that's between you and your Maker, but my guess is no.

The second passage is from Acts 2. You knew I was going to go there, didn't you? Regarding the early church, Luke wrote, "All who believed were together and had all things in common. And they were selling their possessions and belongings and distributing the proceeds to all, as any had need" (vv. 44–45). In both of these New Testament examples, the believer doesn't just give 10%, but is willing to part with everything for the sake of Christ. Such is the attitude one must have when following Jesus. As he said, "If anyone would come after me, let him deny himself and take up his cross daily and follow me" (Lk. 9:23). Picking up a cross means dying to the things of this world. It requires a willingness to forsake your life for Jesus. And how much more valuable is a life than a few pieces of green paper?

Although I don't think the Old Testament directives regarding tithes are in force to those covered under the blood of Christ, I do believe the principles behind tithing are sound and should be followed. Katie and I have tithed for over sixteen years, and we have never regretted it.

Are you put off by the number ten? Don't think you can afford it? Try 5% and go from there. The key here, as with many things in life, is to be consistent. Don't try to give a gift here or there; instead, set aside a percentage of money every time you get paid.

Why Not Prescribe a Number?

I believe God wants people to give of their own volition according to the dictates of their conscience in conjunction with the moving of the Holy Spirit. A prescribed number would seem more like a tax than an offering. And, while it's certainly the Lord's prerogative to levy any demands he desires from his people, he wants our gifts to come from the heart. As Paul taught the Corinthians, "Each one must give as he has decided in his heart, not reluctantly or under compulsion, for God loves a cheerful giver" (2 Cor. 9:7).

On the other end of the spectrum, recovering Pharisees like myself would be tempted to try to justify themselves by their gifts. Those who gave the prescribed 10% would feel justified and righteous before God when, in reality, we know that we are only justified by Jesus's blood through his atoning sacrifice. The tithers could also use such a rubric to look down upon those who fail to give as much. In addition, a 10% prescription might actually limit some people's generosity. Those who might otherwise give 15% or 20% or more might not give as much had Jesus prescribed a tithe.

Last, I think it's important to give to your tithe to the local church. The church is the vessel Jesus established to carry forward the gospel, so it's important that we support it. Just as Israel was to give a tenth to the Levites who served God, in the same way we should support the body of Christ. And, in supporting the church, we're helping move the kingdom forward, reaching the world with the love of Jesus.

Why Jacob?

So you can see Proverbs has quite a bit of wisdom to offer one wishing to receive blessings, but, as promised, let's return to Psalm 24:3–6:

> *Who shall ascend the hill of the LORD?*
> *And who shall stand in his holy place?*
> *He who has clean hands and a pure heart,*
> *who does not lift up his soul to what is false*
> *and does not swear deceitfully.*
> *He will receive blessing from the LORD*
> *and righteousness from the God of his salvation.*
> *Such is the generation of those who seek him,*
> *who seek the face of the God of Jacob.*

At the outset of this chapter, I wrote that three things stood out to me from this passage. For the third noteworthy item, we need to concentrate on the last verse of this passage. David wrote that those who receive God's blessings are of the generation "who seek him." We examined this endeavor at length in part one, so we are well acquainted with seeking God out. Yet verse six contains an interesting phrase. The psalmist claims those who seek God will receive his blessing, but he also offers the descriptor, "the God of Jacob." Seems a bit odd, doesn't it, to bring Jacob into all of this?[40]

Maybe I'm reading too much into this passage. After all, the book of Psalms does use the phrase "God of Jacob" thirteen other times. Nevertheless, I think mentioning Jacob was deliberate. David could have said "God of Abraham" or "God of Isaac." Of course, Jacob was the father of God's people—the twelve tribes of Israel. But why not, then, write "the God of Israel?" But even if I am inserting my own bias into this verse, it is still interesting to examine Jacob in this context.

If you know anything about Jacob, you know he has a sordid past when it comes to blessings. When his father, Isaac, was elderly, blind, and on the brink of death, he called for Esau, his firstborn, to bring him wild game so he could bless the hairy red man. Rebekah overheard Isaac's command, and Jacob, with his mom's help, tricked Isaac into giving him his blessing. To do so, Jacob dressed himself from Esau's wardrobe and laid the skin of young goats on his arms to simulate Esau's hairiness. Rebekah prepared the meal, and Jacob brought it to his father. When he came in to Isaac, Isaac asked, "'Who are you, my son?' Jacob said to his father, 'I am Esau your firstborn'"

---

[40] We must acknowledge the funky language of this verse and translation efforts thereof. The Masoretic text—the Hebrew manuscripts on which we base our Old Testament—doesn't actually include the words "God of." A more faithful translation would be something like, "who seek the face of God, Jacob." Scholars borrowed from the Septuagint—the Greek translation of the Old Testament—to supply the apparent missing words.

(Gen. 27:18–19). After a while, Isaac again asked, "Are you really my son Esau?" (v. 24). Jacob again claimed to be his brother.

Rebekah's plan worked. Jacob received his father's blessing, to the chagrin of Isaac and the ire of Esau (so much that Esau planned on killing his brother after their father passed). But if this ugly incident weren't enough, Jacob gives us another cautionary tale. Fast forward a few years, and we see an impending confrontation between Esau and Jacob. The younger had fled at the advice of Mom-of-the-Year Rebekah, who knew of Esau's murderous intentions and wanted Jacob to find a wife among Rebekah's family.

Jacob traveled northeast to Haran, where God indeed blessed him. He ended up with flocks, wealth, and offspring. He became so wealthy, in fact, that his uncle/father-in-law, Laban, "did not regard him with favor as before" (31:2). So God told him to pack up and return home to the land of Canaan. There was one problem with that command, though. Esau still haunted those parts and, last Jacob knew, wanted to kill him. Nevertheless, Jacob obeyed, running away yet again. As Jacob neared the Jordan River, he divided his camp in two so that if his brother attacked one, the other would escape. He sent messengers with lavish gifts to appease Esau. He waited until night and sent his camp and family across the river Jabbok, a tributary of the Jordan, but stayed behind by himself.[41]

Maybe you know this story. A "man" came and wrestled with Jacob all night. As day broke, the man (purportedly an angel) dislocated Jacob's hip since he could not overcome Jacob. Do you remember what Jacob did? He latched onto the man. Then the man pleaded:

"Let me go, for the day has broken." But Jacob said, "I will not let you go unless you bless me." And he said to him, "What

---

[41] See Genesis 32:22–24.

is your name?" And he said, "Jacob." Then he said, "Your name shall no longer be called Jacob, but Israel."
Genesis 32:26–28

Here we see Jacob, again, striving for a blessing. When before he received blessing by trickery, here he attempts to gain blessing by force. In the midst of the struggle, the man asks Jacob an odd question: "What is your name?" If it seems random, it's not. This isn't the first time someone asked Jacob his name. Remember what Isaac asked when Jacob came to him for the blessing pretending to be Esau? Isaac asked, "Who are you, my son?" To which Jacob lied and claimed to be his brother. So here, the agent of God gave Jacob a test to see if he would own his identity. He gave him a shot a redemption.

We should take a moment here to examine the meaning of the name Jacob. The name sounds like the Hebrew word for heel.[42] Rebekah gave him this name because at his birth, Jacob grasped the heel of his twin brother. It's as if Jacob was trying to pull Esau back so he could be born first and receive the rights thereof. So while the name Jacob might literally mean something like "heel-grabber," it carries with it a deeper meaning of *supplanter*, or, as the NIV footnote more bluntly states it, *cheater*. The idea here is of one who grabs the heel of another to trip him up in order to gain an advantage. Indeed, after Jacob tricked his dad and Esau discovered what happened, Esau said, "Is he not rightly named Jacob? For he has cheated me these two times. He took away my birthright, and behold, now he has taken

---

[42] Herbert E. Ryle, *The Book of Genesis*, The Cambridge Bible for Schools and Colleges, (London: Cambridge University Press, 1921), 270, digitized online edition, https://babel.hathitrust.org/cgi/pt?id=mdp.39015039361004&view=1up&seq=348.

away my blessing" (27:36). This might seem like a cruel thing to name your child, but Rebekah had some spiritual insight regarding her boys. Prior to giving birth, the Lord told Rebekah that "Two nations are in your womb, and two peoples from within you shall be divided; the one shall be stronger than the other, the older shall serve the younger" (25:23). This last phrase is unusual since all of the rights and authority would normally be the domain of the eldest son. So with this insight in mind, the heel grasping was the beginning of the fulfillment of prophecy that Jacob would do whatever he could to supplant his older brother.

So when the angel asked Jacob his name, it was a test to see if Jacob would own up to his own treachery and deceitfulness. This time, instead of pretending to be someone or something he wasn't, he gave the man his rightful name, which doubled as a confession: *I am the cheater.* Immediately, the angel changed his name to Israel, effectively relieving him of his past sins and identity. Then, as verse 29 tells us, "He blessed him."

So with this context in mind, let's go back to the psalm:

> *He will receive blessing from the LORD*
> *and righteousness from the God of his salvation.*
> *Such is the generation of those who seek him,*
> *who seek the face of the God of Jacob.*

It may seem odd or even random to bring Jacob into this, but I believe it is very much purposeful. You see, on the surface, it appears that Jacob succeeded in receiving two blessings by his own machinations—deceiving his father and extorting an angel. In the former instance, this is true. He received his father's blessings by pretending to be someone he wasn't. Yet in the latter, God blessed Jacob despite his efforts. The angel didn't bless Jacob so that Jacob would let him free. Rather, he waited until Jacob owned his identity and his troubled past to give him his blessing.

This psalm, in the context of Jacob's shortcomings, reminds us that although we might be able to receive earthly riches by deceit, real lasting blessings come from above—not from any of our futile efforts. Put another way, you don't have to pretend you're someone you're not to receive God's blessings. In reality, God wants to bless all people, but it requires answering the question Jacob lied about the first time but owned the second time: "Who are you? What is your name?" When we admit who we are, when we own our identities as imperfect, fallen, and sinful humans, God gives us a new identity in Christ.

To receive God's blessings, then, we must seek out the God of Jacob. In referencing Jacob, maybe David is reminding us that God is a god of second chances and a god who can transform who we are into someone he wants us to be. Maybe it is a reminder that God still loved and blessed Jacob, one of the biggest screwups in all of the Bible, not because Jacob earned or deserved it but because God is good and wants to bless his people. We need only to admit we're a bunch of heel-grabbers and turn to him for what we need.

CHAPTER 6
Is It Okay to Prosper?

*Why is it that the only blessing of God that we
apologize for is wealth?*
—Craig Groeschel[43]

Viewing blessings through the lens of eternity changes our
perspective on prosperity.

If you were to stop reading this book right now, you would no doubt walk away with some important keys to the Christian life and experience divine blessings. Nevertheless, stopping at this point would be a disservice because we are leaving several critical questions regarding money and Christianity unanswered. Of course, as you know, blessing and money are not synonyms, but since wealth can be one form of blessing, we often intertwine the two. As a result, it is necessary that we address some misconceptions and falsehoods surrounding God's blessings. Specifically, let's examine three unbiblical beliefs about money.

---

[43] As quoted in Ramsey, *The Legacy Journey*, location 324 of 2961.

1. God is obligated to bless you if you give.

The first thing we must clear up is this: God is *not* obligated to bless you just because you give. In the previous chapter, we discussed the importance of generosity as a characteristic of those whom God blesses. Nevertheless, giving simply to get totally misses the point. God blesses the generous because he is generous. As we learn to give more, we become more like Jesus, who gave it all. That in itself is a blessing, because everything about God is good. Even still, God does bless those who seek after him. Part of doing so is by living generous lives. But operating with the premise that God must bless us because we give is backwards thinking. In this mentality, we set ourselves and God up in a type of employer-employee relationship rather than father-child or creator-created relationship.

You see, as an employee, I give something of myself: my time, my services, my sweat, and my mental fortitude. By the end of most days in my Information Technology job, my brain is exhausted. But why do I give so much of myself for eight hours a day five days a week? I do so in return for a paycheck. My employer and I have an agreement. I render them services and they pay me. Therefore, as long as I keep up my end of the bargain, our arrangement obligates them to pay me the amount they said they would on the day they said they would. All good capitalists are familiar with this model. It's natural. It's logical.

But problems abound when we start treating God like an employer. *I gave my tithe. I sponsored a child in Ethiopia. I emptied out my wallet for that homeless guy. I did what you said, God; I was generous. Now bless me immeasurably.* Do you see how this misses the point entirely? In this type of relationship, the employer needs something from his employees. He needs help running the business, flipping burgers, or repairing computers, so the organization hires people to meet its needs. God, on the other hand, needs nothing. As we said in chapter five, God doesn't need a thing from you. As the Scripture says, "Every beast of the forest is [God's], the cattle on a thousand hills" (Ps. 50:10). He created time and space and matter, and yet we think he might need our generosity? It's ludicrous. No, God commands generosity because it is good for us and it is good for other people he loves. As Jesus said, "It is better to give than to receive."[44]

Now, some might say, "This is all true, and God really doesn't need anything from us, but God obligated himself by his promises of blessings." Now we're getting somewhere. The origin of this line of thinking can often be traced to verses like Malachi 3:10, which reads, "'Bring the whole tithe into the storehouse, that there may be food in my house. Test me in this,' says the LORD Almighty, 'and see if I will not throw open the floodgates of heaven and pour out so much blessing that there will not be room enough to store it.'" I love this verse and verses like it, and I think the principle behind these promises do still apply today. But I also think it is important to remember that through these prophets, God spoke to a specific people in a specific context. Plucking these verses out of the text without a larger understanding of what's going on in the passage can be dangerous.

Aside from that, there's a nuance here, something that is overlooked by many. Notice what God says through Malachi. He will open up the floodgates of heaven. Translation: he will make it rain. Of what use is the rain if you haven't done the hard work of preparing the ground and planting the seeds? You might desire fruit, but all you'll get is mud.

That's the mistake some Christians make. They think it's enough to give money to God, and then they can just kick back and wait for

---

[44] As quoted in Acts 20:35.

the checks to roll in. The question is this: If God sent you rain, would you be ready for it? You must be generous toward God, but you also must work hard. Neglect either of these, and you'll be left wondering why God isn't blessing you.

Of course, we don't (or shouldn't) give just to get something in return. That's idiotic. That's manipulative. I'm sure you've met someone like that before. He's scummy and slimy. No, we give because Jesus gave it all at Calvary. We give because that's who our God is and we want to be like him. God loves to bless his children, but he's not going to bless you if you're stingy, lazy, or manipulative.

2. If you follow God, you'll become rich.

The second misconception follows in a similar vein as the first. It's easy to shoot down, but sadly, many churches around the world preach this "prosperity" message: Following God leads to earthly riches. True, many Old Testament patriarchs like Abraham, Isaac, and Jacob all became very wealthy as a blessing from God. Joseph became rich and powerful. David and Solomon too.

But when you get to the New Testament, many Christ followers were poor. There were some rich converts like Lydia and Cornelius, but they represented the minority. After Jesus suggested the rich young ruler sell his possessions, Peter said to Jesus, "We have left everything to follow you!" (Matt. 19:27). And Jesus himself left no material inheritance. The Roman soldiers gambled for his clothing—his only earthly possessions—as he suffocated on the cross.

Furthermore, confessing Christ in the three centuries following Jesus's death was no picnic. The Roman Empire vacillated between ambivalence and outright hostility toward this new religion under the helm of emperors like Nero and Decius until Christianity became Rome's official religion in 313 AD. Following Jesus in these times sometimes led to things much worse than destitution. The Roman historian and politician Tacitus wrote that Nero blamed Christians for the Great Fire of Rome in 64 AD:

> *Nero fastened the guilt and inflicted the most exquisite tortures on a class hated for their abominations, called Christians by the populace. . . Mockery of every sort was added to their deaths. Covered with the skins of beasts, they were torn by dogs and perished, or were nailed to crosses, or were doomed to the flames and burnt, to serve as a nightly illumination, when daylight had expired.[45]*

In his first epistle, the apostle Peter wrote that it is beneficial to suffer for good deeds, claiming, "For to this you have been called, because Christ also suffered for you, leaving you an example, so that you might follow in his steps" (1 Pet. 2:21). Nero's persecution of Christians is just one such example.

Even today in first-world countries we see examples all around us of Christians who struggle with finances, which pales in comparison, of course, to those in third-world nations and nations in which Christianity is illegal, but it is still antithetical to the argument that followers of Christ will be wealthy.

When one operates under the assumption that all Christians will become rich, it forces him or her to come to difficult conclusions when faced with any of these counter-examples. These range from the dubious "she doesn't have enough faith" to the accusatory "he has sin in his life." The latter is the exact argument we encounter in John 9 when the disciples see a man "blind from birth" and ask Jesus,

---

[45] Tacitus, *The Annals*, Book XV,
http://classics.mit.edu/Tacitus/annals.11.xv.html.

"Rabbi, who sinned, this man or his parents, that he was born blind?" (v. 2). Jesus, though, challenged their presuppositions and told them, "It was not that this man sinned, or his parents, but that the works of God might be displayed in him" (v. 3). Then Jesus restored the man's sight.

Sometimes God has plans for his followers other than earthly riches, but make no mistake, he knows what's best for us. I believe God does financially bless many of his followers, especially those who are faithful in managing money, but coming to Christ isn't a guarantee of earthly wealth.

3. Rich people are evil.

No doubt you've also encountered this last falsehood regarding Christians and their relationships to money: rich people are evil. Such a statement would be laughable were it not so prevalent in the world today. This is the opposite pendulum swing from the previous misconception and very popular in US political discourse these days: if you have money, that means you stole it, cheated someone out of it, or hurt someone to get it.

This argument is usually fueled by misquotations of Scripture and a selective look at what Jesus said about money. Jesus did say it's easier for a camel to go through the eye of a needle than for a rich man to enter heaven (Matt. 19:24). But guess what? It's impossible for *anyone* to enter heaven on his or her own merit. I think this is the point Jesus was making: Money can't buy you eternity or favor with God. What about the rich young ruler? Jesus told him to sell everything and give the proceeds to the poor, so everyone should do that, right? And this proves money is evil, right?

Truth is, the young man had a heart condition in regard to money. He loved it and couldn't let go. Maybe you *should* sell everything you own and give it to the poor. That could be tremendously admirable. But if you have a healthy, godly relationship with cash, God's probably not asking you to do so.

Money is amoral. Whether you're worth $1 billion or you're drowning in debt, God loves you the same. It's your attitude toward money that counts.

Is It Wrong to Want to Be Rich?

In the previous chapter, we learned how to receive God's blessings. But in light of these three misconceptions, we must ask: is it wrong to want to be rich? But before we can even attempt to answer this question, we must ask another: how much money makes someone "rich?"

If your net worth is $50,000, you'd probably say $500,000.

If your net worth is $500,000, you'd probably say $5 million.

Five million? $50 million. And so on.

When you ask someone how much it takes to be wealthy, chances are they'll say, "More than I have right now." Few people identify themselves as rich.

Recently, I read 1 Timothy 6. You know, the chapter from which we get the infamous (and often misquoted) verse "The love of money is a root of all kinds of evils" (1 Tim. 6:10). But what caught my attention this time around was the preceding verse: "Those who want to get rich fall into temptation and a trap and into many foolish and harmful desires that plunge people into ruin and destruction" (v. 9 NIV).

Katie and I have taught money guru Dave Ramsey's financial course a couple of times. If you've been through the material, you know that the last of his steps is "Build Wealth and Give." But doesn't this pursuit to build wealth contradict Paul's admonition to

Timothy? Should your goal be to build wealth if "those who want to get rich fall into temptation?"

The Truth about Being Rich

There's a subtle but real difference between wanting to build wealth and wanting to get rich. Do you see it? The former is something you do, an activity: I build wealth. The latter is something you become: I am rich. Getting rich is about identity. It's about wanting money to change who you are. As I said above, the amount of money you have does not matter because money is amoral. The problem arises when we allow our bank accounts to define us. As a result, we must be careful to distinguish between pursuing wealth and the pursuit of becoming wealthy. If that sounds like splitting hairs, it's because the line between the two can often become blurry. So just remember this: your attitude toward money is what counts. Christians who desire to get rich are missing the point.

They are already rich.

Whatever your finances look like, whatever your net worth, if Christ is in your life, you're filthy rich. That's why Paul says that the desire to get rich plunges you "into ruin and destruction." In failing to recognize the riches you already have, you seek abundance and security from external sources rather than from God. Deriving our identities from anything other than God and our relationship to him is wrong. That, of course, includes money. Yes, I'm a father, brother, son, husband, IT professional, author, homeowner, Oklahoman, and darn good barbecuer. But these are all secondary to my identity in Christ. I'm a Christian first. I'm a child of God. That makes me the richest kid on earth. So to desire to become rich is idiotic because it pushes God out of the frame and replaces him with money. In doing so, we become John Doe, billionaire, instead of John Doe, son of

God. If you had to pick, which one would you choose?

So what Paul's really writing about in 1 Timothy 6 is not the evils of being rich, but rather about the evils of not being content. As he wrote in the passage, "godliness with contentment is great gain" (v. 6). And this sense of contentment is not just with what we have, but also with who we are. Often, the desire for riches demonstrates a lack on contentment with our identity in Christ. We are not content with Jesus; we want more. This is a sin. We think there's room for money up there on the pedestal of identity, so we strive to become a rich Christian. But Christ must be above all.

Jesus said, "No one can serve two masters. Either you will hate the one and love the other, or you will be devoted to the one and despise the other. You cannot serve both God and money" (Matt. 6:24 NIV). So is it wrong to want to be rich? If you're a Christian, the question self-destructs. It's invalid. Because if you're a Christian, you already are.

We Still Worship Gold

Not long after the Israelites' miraculous exodus from Egypt, Moses went up to the top of Mount Sinai to receive instruction from God. On top of Sinai for forty days and nights, Moses received the Ten Commandments and various other laws for the Israelites to follow.[46] Down at the bottom of the mountain, from the people's perspective, the mountain appeared as if it were on fire.

Those forty days must have seemed like decades to the Israelites, who waited anxiously for their leader to return. Hours turned to days. Days to weeks. But as the weeks turned to months, the rumblings began. *Moses must have lost favor with God. God must have consumed*

---

[46] See Exodus 24:18.

him in his holy fire. What else could they assume? They hadn't heard a peep from their leader, the man who drew them out of Egypt to freedom. But they couldn't wait forever. They would die in the desert. So they went to the second-in-command.

To Aaron, Moses's brother, they said, "Up, make us gods who shall go before us. As for this Moses, the man who brought us up out of the land of Egypt, we do not know what has become of him" (Ex. 32:1). Aaron, probably also wondering what had happened to Moses, obliged. He collected gold from the people and, after melting it, formed the precious metal into the image of a calf. *Israel, meet your new god.*

Moses, as you know, wasn't dead. After wrapping up his Law 101 semester with Yahweh, he descended the mountain, stone tablets in hand. At the sight of the idol, Moses became furious and hurled the tablets, breaking them.

Through the eyes of your average post-enlightenment twenty-first-century Christian, this is one of the most incredulous stories in all of Scripture. What morons! God had done incredible things for Israel in Egypt. He had sent plagues like darkness, frogs, and lice and parted the Red Sea for them to cross to safety. He delivered them from the angel of death on the night of Passover and led them to freedom. How quickly they forgot. If that wasn't enough, the very gold they used to create the calf came because of God's provision. As Exodus 12 relates the story:

> *The people of Israel had also done as Moses told them, for they had asked the Egyptians for silver and gold jewelry and for clothing. And the LORD had given the people favor in the sight of the Egyptians, so that they let them have what they asked. Thus they plundered the Egyptians.*
> Exodus 12:35–36

How crazy are these people? And yet, as much as this story offends our intellects, in reality, we still worship gold too—just in different ways. Our methods might be more subtle than melting down jewelry to form the image of a calf, but the end result is the same: the glorification of wealth for purposes of security, entertainment, or esteem. (Note: when I write "we" and "our," I don't mean to single out readers of this book, but rather to indicate Western society as a whole. You might not have this problem at all, but the culture in which we find ourselves certainly does. And I would be lying were I to claim that I have never struggled with modern-day gold worship.)

If you need examples, simply turn on the television. Countless programs featured in streaming services and cable channels allow viewers to access the lives of the wealthy. In the 1980s and 90s, audiences lapped up the Robin Leach-hosted *Lifestyles of the Rich and Famous*. The decade-plus tenure of the program demonstrates America's fascination with opulent and over-the-top lifestyles. As Leach himself said, "No one would watch 'Lifestyles of the Poor and Unknown.'"[47]

But *Lifestyles* is just one in a long line of "reality" shows glorifying the wealthy and inviting viewers into their lives. How do we explain the success of such programming? The primary appeal is to cathartic wish fulfillment. It's fun to imagine life lived with excess and luxury. This trend isn't just relegated to television either. Publications like *Us Weekly* exist for the sole purpose of slaking society's thirst for intricate details of celebrity lives, and social media has given rise to even more celebrities and more access than ever before.

If it sounds like I'm judging, well, maybe I am a little. But I'm

---

[47] Neil Genzlinger, "Robin Leach, 76, 'Lifestyles of the Rich and Famous' Host, Dies," New York Times, August 24, 2018, https://www.nytimes.com/2018/08/24/obituaries/robin-leach-dead-lifestyles-rich-famous.html.

not immune either. I enjoy watching shows in which people buy vacation homes in gorgeous locations. Why? Because I can imagine myself in one of those homes. It's fun to picture what life would be like living in the Virgin Islands.

Yet this obsession with the wealthy betrays our penchant for gold worship. No, it's not the same as bowing down to a golden calf, but is it so dissimilar? The Israelites were afraid because Moses had been up on the mountain for a long time. They thought God had abandoned them and they would be vulnerable in the wilderness without his protection. So they fashioned their own god in want of security. In the West, we worship money for the security we believe it will provide us. With enough money, we think we'll never be caught off guard in the wilderness. Money can buy security systems, armed guards, life and disability insurance policies, lawyers, firearms, and the best physicians. This, I think, is the real reason we still worship gold. We think if we have enough in our bank accounts, we won't have to rely on God for his provision and protection. Or, at least, we'll have a backup plan in case God doesn't come through for us.

Why Not Let God Fulfill Your Needs?

Security isn't the only reason people worship money today. For some, money represents endless entertainment: yachts, vacations, concerts, and sporting events. For others, wealth funds the pursuit of esteem. We all desire respect, but some crave to be awed by others. Money, so the thinking goes, can garner the esteem of mankind. And while money can purchase some measure of all three of these things—security, entertainment, and esteem—these things are all temporary, fragile, and, by and large, illegitimate. Jesus taught on this in the Sermon on the Mount. He said:

Do not lay up for yourselves treasures on earth, where moth and rust destroy and where thieves break in and steal, but lay up for yourselves treasures in heaven, where neither moth nor rust destroys and where thieves do not break in and steal. For where your treasure is, there your heart will be also.
Matthew 6:19–21

No matter how much money you have, those possessions are vulnerable to the corrupted nature of the universe. Earthly riches are finite and temporary. Nevertheless, all three of these desires are legitimate expressions of the human heart. We should not feel guilty about seeking out security or even entertainment or esteem. As the famous psychologist Abraham Maslow taught, security is a fundamental need of the human condition.[48] Without it, few other needs can be met. In addition, we all need fun and diversion from time to time to refresh our bodies and our minds. God did not create us to be robotic in our approach to life. Jesus spent many days eating and drinking with his friends like Lazarus in Bethany. For example, read what Jesus said to the Pharisees who were critical of his choices: "The Son of Man has come eating and drinking, and you say, 'Look at him! A glutton and a drunkard, a friend of tax collectors and sinners!'" (Lk. 7:34).

Even esteem is a legitimate desire. We all want to feel loved and important to others. We all want respect. The problem with this and other needs comes when we do not allow God to fulfill them. When we turn to money for security rather than God, that's a sin. (And it's stupid too.) If you seek entertainment outside of the boundaries God has set in place, that's a sin. And God should be your source of esteem and belonging.

---

[48] Saul McLeod, "Maslow's Hierarchy of Needs," Simply Psychology, December 29, 2020, https://www.simplypsychology.org/maslow.html.

Blessing, Defined

With these myths and biases about money laid bare, perhaps it would be helpful to back up and define blessing in the modern context, since the word can mean many different things and since it looks way different than it did for the Hebrew forefathers in the Ancient Near East.

Merriam-Webster's dictionary lends the following: "a thing conducive to happiness or welfare."[49] The temptation for me (and, I think, the world in general) is to think of blessings only in financial terms. This was especially true for the Hebrew people throughout much of biblical history. While their views on the afterlife are unclear, the Tanakh, and especially the Torah (the first five books of the Tanakh), is mostly silent on whether we persist after we die. By the first century, the debate among Jews continued. The New Testament tells us that the Sadducees did not believe in resurrection while the Pharisees did.[50] With this context in mind, you can see how people could take a narrow view of blessing. If there is nothing beyond death, there can exist no transcendent, eternal blessings—no moral victories or growth opportunities that could serve you for all time. Instead, blessings were a rather clear-cut matter: physical wealth in the form of money, animals, servants, and land; health; peace from enemies; a large family. The general belief went like this: God blesses the upright and brings ruin to the dishonest and lazy. Yet, as we saw with Jacob, you can do just about everything wrong and still receive God's blessing. And, in the case of Job, you can do just about everything right and still see ruin. But despite these cautionary tales on either side, these beliefs about blessing persisted to New

---

[49] Merriam-Webster, s.v. "blessing," accessed January 22, 2021, https://www.merriam-webster.com/dictionary/blessing.
[50] See Matthew 22:23 for one example.

Testament times, leading the disciples, at the sight of a blind man, to ask Jesus, "Who sinned, this man or his parents, that he was born blind?" (Jn. 9:2). In their minds, there could be no other explanation for a man who was blind. Jesus of course, set them straight: "It was not that this man sinned, or his parents, but that the works of God might be displayed in him" (v. 3).

When Jesus taught the Sermon on the Mount in Matthew 5, he turned the notion of blessing on its head. In one of the most radical speeches of all time, Jesus began to undo popular misconceptions surrounding the subject. He said things like "Blessed are the poor in spirit" and "Blessed are those who mourn" (vv. 3, 4). Without the promise of eternity, these statements would ring hollow. But in light of eternity, we have the promise of restoration and glory with God in heaven. As Jesus said in conclusion to the Beatitudes regarding those who are persecuted, "Rejoice and be glad, for your reward is great in heaven" (v. 12). Jesus here redefines blessing, teaching that the best rewards come to us in heaven. Earthly wealth is temporary, but heavenly blessings are forever.

Therefore, it is folly to think of blessing only in financial terms, since we have the promise of eternal life in Jesus Christ. As James wrote, "Every good gift and every perfect gift is from above, coming down from the Father" (1:17). Therefore, every good thing we receive comes from God. He cannot give bad gifts, and we cannot receive anything good that has not originated from our heavenly Father.

Some of the greatest blessings are those we take for granted every day—things like our health. Spend some time with someone struggling with a chronic medical condition and ask him or her the value of wellness. We tend to overlook blessings like clean drinking water, electricity, religious freedom, and a myriad of other things. Even things that seem bad at the time can become blessings in the long run. How many times have you heard stories of someone fired from his job who reflects in retrospect, "That was the best thing that ever happened to me"?

The best blessing is the rest we receive through our assurance of salvation and eternity with Jesus. The author of Hebrews, speaking of heaven, wrote, "There remains a Sabbath rest for the people of God, for whoever has entered God's rest has also rested from his works as God did from his" (4:9–10). One day, we will have rest from laboring against nature, from working against the second law of thermodynamics. The Christian can live free of anxiety of death, secure in his or her postmortem destiny thanks to the sacrifice Jesus made on the cross. As a result, we can endure periods of mourning and times of persecution and actually consider them blessings—as backwards as that sounds—knowing that Jesus can and will restore all things and even reward those who suffer for his name.

So we can see that blessings come in many forms, but let's steer back to finances for a moment. Is it okay for the Christian to prosper? Should one feel guilty for achieving financial success?

Some may cite the example of the rich young man who was directed by Jesus to sell his possessions. But remember, this guy's problem was the same as the Israelites' problem, and the same as we see in our culture today. He worshiped his gold. He loved the security and esteem his wealth provided him. It made the young man feel fuzzy inside. If you have the same problem—if you worship your wealth, if you love the security and status it provides you—then please sell it all right now. Again, God is our one and only source of security, and the only status that ultimately matters is our relationship with him.

Remember that God's gifts are good and God loves to bless his children. Does this mean that every Christian should be wealthy? That those who aren't wealthy simply don't have enough faith? Of course not. But many Christians have become wealthy by adhering to the principles of the previous chapter: integrity, hard work, a thirst for wisdom, and generosity. Where's the shame in that?

If you have obtained wealth by unethical means or if you are stingy with what you have, then yes, go ahead and feel guilty for your prosperity. Unethical people get rich every day. But that money isn't a blessing for those people. Instead, it serves as a magnifying glass to enlarge the wickedness in their hearts. But if you've lived your life faithful in the little things, don't be surprised if God gives you even more to manage for the kingdom. He wants you to be wildly rich, even if that means waiting until after this life to receive his eternal riches.

CHAPTER 7
Stop Reading Proverbs

In much wisdom is much vexation, and he who increases
knowledge increases sorrow.
—King Solomon[51]

Reading the book of Proverbs in a vacuum leads only to
disillusionment and bad theology.

Proverbs is a wonderful book. The work, primarily written and compiled by King Solomon,[52] doles out solid advice for everyday life. With guidance such as "Whoever loves discipline loves knowledge, but he who hates reproof is stupid" (12:1) and "A man without self-control is like a city broken into and left without walls" (25:28), how could one argue?

The thesis of the book could be summed up in chapter one verse seven, in which Solomon writes, "The fear of the LORD is the beginning of knowledge." Therefore, by God, do everything in your power to obtain and heed wisdom, because if you do, you will prosper. Meanwhile, fools and the wicked (synonymous to Solomon)

---

[51] Ecclesiastes 1:18.

[52] It appears that Solomon borrowed from some other world philosophers.

will see ruin. The traits of the Proverbs fool involve any combination of the following descriptors: stingy, lazy, violent, dishonest, a gossiper, and an adulterer. In essence, the argument of the book is this: You will reap what you sow, so sow wisdom since it will yield riches, honor, long life, contentment, and a host of other things.

As you progress through this chapter and the rest of this book, please understand that I love the book of Proverbs. It is uplifting, hopeful, and insightful. The aphorisms contained in the chapters are timeless and still applicable to this very day. Nevertheless, there lies a danger in reading Proverbs on its own—without the context of the Gospels and even other wisdom literature in the Old Testament. Put simply, it is unwise to base your entire worldview on the book of Proverbs.

Now, you might be thinking I'm silly even to bring up such a notion. Surely no one out there reads only the book of Proverbs and derives all truth about living from that book. I hope you're right. You probably are. Nevertheless, even among those who do regularly read and study the Bible, it seems as if there's a faction of people who operate as if the Proverbs are the ultimate source of knowledge for daily living.

Have you ever seen those tiny Bibles people pass out on college campuses and at other public places? I got one myself several years ago as a student at the University of Oklahoma. Mine is green with an imitation-leather feel to the cover, and it is printed on that extra-thin paper you see in dictionaries. If you've been alive for a few years, you've probably seen these out in the wild. I love mine because it fits neatly into my pocket for easy transportation. Most of my Scripture reading is digital these days, but I still hang on to that pocket Bible for times when I need a paper copy on the go.

The idea behind these Bibles is to get God's Word into the hands of as many people as possible, so The Gideons International organization makes them small. That way, they're cheaper to produce and they won't overwhelm people who may not be familiar with the Bible. As a result, they exclude the entire Old Testament except for two books. Know what those books are? Psalms and Proverbs. Why include these two from the Old Testament? Why not Genesis? Haggai? Zephaniah?

Psalms needs no defense. Among Jesus's Tanakh quotations, Psalms tops the list of most-quoted books. Even on the cross, he shouted out a psalm: "My God, my God, why have you forsaken me?" (22:1). So that leaves Proverbs. Why include it as one of only two of the thirty-nine Old Testament books included in the Gideon Bible? One obvious answer is that it is a standalone book. There's no narrative, no larger story you need to understand to read the book. And yet the same could be said about Ecclesiastes. But Ecclesiastes is just depressing. Bingo. Now we're on to something. Proverbs is uplifting. It is encouraging. It makes sense to the reader; if I don't talk poorly about people, they will be more likely to trust and respect me. If I work diligently in the summer, I'll reap a harvest in the fall. No duh. But if these arguments are so obvious, why do we need to read them?

Let's go back to the second law of thermodynamics and our brains for a moment. Remember, our brains are lazy, doing everything they can to preserve energy to ensure survival because they are subconsciously aware of the second law and the impending heat death of the universe. As futile as it may be, our brains are trying to decrease entropy so we will have enough energy to survive. As a result, we feel tempted at every turn to please our brains. This involves doing what feels good: cutting corners, talking poorly about people we don't like, sleeping in when we should be hitting the fields, committing adultery, eating too much food, and so on. This is the corrupted nature of the human condition and we, as Christians, must actively fight against it every day. The person who thinks he or she is immune is the most vulnerable of us all. The book of Proverbs, then, fills this hole, guiding us, prodding us, and reminding us of the importance of fearing God and living upright lives. Those who do, Solomon says, "will flourish" (14:11).

So far so good, right? You're reading Proverbs. You're pumped up. You've been giving generously to God, living with integrity as best as you can, and working hard. But one day you don't feel so well, so you call in sick. Your stomach is killing you, and your back hurts too. *Maybe it's just the atomic burrito I ate last night*, you think. You feel a little better the next day, but as the days wear on, you notice you've lost ten pounds in a couple of weeks and you're tired all the time no matter what you do. Finally, you visit your doctor. The CT scan confirms it: pancreatic cancer. Terminal. Twelve months to live, tops. Doing your best to cope with your newfound death sentence, you pick up your Bible. In your quiet time you read Proverbs 9:11: "For by [wisdom] your days will be multiplied, and years will be added to your life."

You've got twelve months left to live. How can this be true?

Or say you've been following the four-step blessing plan from chapter five and you're making progress. Your barns aren't bursting yet, but you're doing better every day. One day, your boss calls you in. No fault of your own, but the company has fallen on some hard times and they've got to lay you off. No severance, no nothing. Just a handshake. And then you read in your Bible, "The hand of the diligent makes rich" (Prov. 10:4).

Do you see the problem?

Now, again, you might think I'm stating the obvious and that no one would turn only to Solomon for life advice. Even if this is true, when things are going well, we have a tendency to focus only on the good, encouraging parts of Scripture. Yes, we read and intellectually incorporate books like Ecclesiastes and Jeremiah, which are full of sorrow and disillusionment. But we read them as if they're only a story and not a commentary on the human condition. I'm generalizing, of course, but you get the point. The tricky thing about Proverbs is that, in general, its principles are spot on. Most of the time its aphorisms hold true.

In fact, as far as we can control things (which isn't as much as we'd like to think), Solomon gives some of the best advice you can find. But we must also examine the book's counterpoints and exceptions lest we descend into anger, despair, and disillusionment when things don't turn out how we expect them to. In reality, bad things do happen to good people. Every day. So, yes, please study and apply the wisdom of Proverbs to your life, but don't do it in a vacuum. Don't read Proverbs without reading its counterpoints. Let's look at two examples: Ecclesiastes and Job.

The Problem of Pleasure

Ecclesiastes is a great place to turn first because the same man responsible for many of the Proverbs also wrote Ecclesiastes. I think this is one of the more important books to read because if you're anything like me, you've had moments when you struggle with meaninglessness. Maybe not on a grand philosophical scale, but in the routine of life. I get up, go to work, do my best, and then repeat it all the next day. My day job is in Information Technology. I'll work all day to resolve one problem and feel satisfied with myself, like I achieved something by resolving a tricky software issue. But then I come in the next day and a host of new problems have arisen. New hardware, new software, new bugs. The cycle is never-ending. As a result, I often feel like a hamster in one of those metal wheels. I run all day only to end up where I started. I feel disheartened that the work I do, ultimately, is meaningless. It's a humbling realization.

No matter what industry you're in or whatever your lot, no doubt you've experienced similar feelings. There's no escaping the consequences of the second law of thermodynamics. As hard as we try to order our universe, there's no stopping the advance of entropy. As you can probably tell, I think about these things quite often in the context of daily life. You can only clean a toilet or pick up a messy room so many times before you start feeling a little insane. How many times can you do the same thing without it feeling pointless? I appreciate clean toilets just as much as the next person, but it is a totally meaningless task. Stand-up comedian Jim Gaffigan has a similar take about making the bed in one of his bits:

> *I don't believe in making the bed, though. My wife's always like, "Why don't you ever make the bed?" For the same reason I don't tie my shoes after I take them off. It doesn't make sense! We're not putting this thing in storage. Hell, I'm hoping to come back in a couple of hours, and I would like it open."*[53]

Joking aside, Gaffigan raises a good point. Why *should* we make the bed? It's just going to get messy again. Why should I mow the yard? The grass will just grow again. Why should I fix that printer? It's just going to break down again eventually. This is why Ecclesiastes is so important. Solomon doesn't shy away from these issues of meaninglessness. He tackles the futile nature of work head-on:

> *Vanity of vanities, says the Preacher,*
> *vanity of vanities! All is vanity.*

---

[53] Jim Gaffigan, "Bed," track 6 on *King Baby*, Comedy Central Records, 2009.

> *What does man gain by all the toil*
> *at which he toils under the sun? . . .*
> *I have seen everything that is done under the sun, and behold,*
> *all is vanity and a striving after wind.*
> Ecclesiastes 1:2–3, 14

That's a lot of vanity. How did we get from "The soul of the sluggard craves and gets nothing, while the soul of the diligent is richly supplied" (Prov. 13:4) to "all is vanity"?

Lonely at the Top

We need to peek into Solomon's life for a moment to understand this contrast. As we saw, Solomon asked for wisdom and God granted it to him in spades. In fact, God told Solomon, "I give you a wise and discerning mind, so that none like you has been before you and none like you shall arise after you" (1 Kgs. 3:12). As a result of asking for wisdom, God blessed him with wealth and peace. Using these resources, Solomon built up an impressive kingdom for himself and for Israel. He executed to perfection his father's plans for the temple and built an impressive palace. He also fortified Jerusalem's wall, built cities, and constructed a fleet of ships in the Red Sea.[54]

Solomon was always in pursuit of the next building project, the next city to bolster, the next army to fortify. Yet with each lofty goal achieved—at the top of the wisdom, wealth, and achievement mountain—Solomon learned how empty these achievements were. They were all vanity.

This is how Solomon arrived at the point where he wrote, "For in much wisdom is much vexation, and he who increases knowledge

---

[54] See 1 Kings 9 for a summary of these projects.

increases sorrow" (Eccl. 1:18). Doesn't this seem like a 180-degree shift from what we see in Proverbs? I thought wisdom was everything?

Solomon tried everything—hard work, alcohol, women, other pleasures—and found all of these pursuits to be lacking. He still felt empty. As he wrote:

> *I said in my heart, "Come now, I will test you with pleasure; enjoy yourself." But behold, this also was vanity. . . . I made great works. I built houses and planted vineyards for myself. I made myself gardens and parks, and planted in them all kinds of fruit trees. . . . Then I considered all that my hands had done and the toil I had expended in doing it, and behold, all was vanity and a striving after wind, and there was nothing to be gained under the sun.*
> Ecclesiastes 2:1, 4–5, 11

This last phrase is key. Solomon discovered that although wisdom and wealth and honor are good things, no amount of any of them can bring meaning *under the sun*. What does that mean? It means on this earth, apart from God. Everything is meaningless without the meaning provided us by our creator. Nothing on this planet could give Solomon the peace and joy he craved.

The same is true for us. Any type of pursuit we might undertake, any possessions or accomplishments we gather are empty and meaningless apart from God.

Job

If Solomon's problem was one of pleasure, Job is a sobering reminder of the problem of pain. Reading Job should be required for anyone with a crush on Proverbs. With each proverb we read, we should also make ourselves examine the boils covering Job's flesh. For every platitude we repeat, we should also echo Job's cries of desperation at the loss of life, property, and health. No, I'm not a masochist, but Job's story provides a critical contrast to the saccharine advice we read in Proverbs.

Again, please don't misread me. I love Proverbs. I think it's an amazing, uplifting book. But reading it without context is like eating only cake for every meal; you're setting yourself up for failure.

As we look at Job, let's start at the end: "The LORD blessed the latter days of Job more than his beginning. And he had 14,000 sheep, 6,000 camels, 1,000 yoke of oxen, and 1,000 female donkeys. He had also seven sons and three daughters" (42:12–13).

The Lord blessed Job. Isn't this what we're after? Yes, but if we had to endure what Job did, I don't think many of us would be quick to sign up. My point is this: those who receive blessings don't always receive them right away, and sometimes those blessings come only after periods of hardship.

But why start at the end of the story? I think too many people overlook this last state of Job. We all know about his suffering and the tragedies he endured, but hear it again: Job was richer than he was prior to losing it all. He was faithful to God, and God honored that. As we enter into this examination of Job and suffering in general, it is important to remember that God has the ability to restore all things. Sometimes, as with Job, that restoration occurs this side of heaven, and sometimes it happens in glory. But it is critical to keep this perspective in mind as we proceed.

But perhaps we *are* getting ahead of ourselves a bit. Let's back up. If you're not familiar with Job, he was a guy who lived "in the land of Uz" (Job 1:1). Uz was mostly likely in Edom, the territory south and east of Jerusalem, home of modern-day Jordan. Genesis tells us of a man named Uz who was a grandson of Seir, a Horite. Uz lived in the region before Esau (also known as Edom) invaded the land. Uz became Esau's uncle-in-law when Esau married Oholibama, the daughter of Anah, the brother of Uz.[55] And, as is common today, cities in the Ancient Near East were often named after their founders, so it is probable that the land of Uz was somewhere in Edom.

When Job lived is a less definite answer. Context clues from the book lend itself to an older date, sometime prior to the Exodus and God's covenant with the Israelites, because Job offered his own sacrifices to God without an intermediary priest.[56] If such is the case, then Job would have had to have lived between approximately 2006 BC (one proposed date for Esau's birth) and the mid-thirteenth century BC (the latest proposed date for the Exodus). In fact, the date could be even later, since Edom remained isolated from the Hebrew people until the conquests of Canaan post-Exodus. Regardless, we know the sixth-century BC prophet Ezekiel knew of Job because Ezekiel mentions him in the fourteenth chapter of his book. So that only leaves about a 1,400-year window in which the man lived. Kind of narrows it down, huh?

That the story escapes proper dating is probably by design due to the timeless message of the work. For our purposes here, the dating of the book of Job isn't critical, but regardless of when it was actually written, it is apparent that the story gained popularity for the exiled Jews in Babylon.[57] Why? Quite simple. It told of a man who lost just about everything and how he endured and persisted in his faith. And in the end, God restored him. Such was the hope of the exiled Jews.

---

[55] See Genesis 36 for details.

[56] Depending on the dating method, the Exodus likely occurred either in the thirteenth century BC (around 1267) or the fifteenth century BC (1446).

[57] *The Chronological Study Bible: New International Version* (Nashville: Thomas Nelson, 2014), location 64160 of 126745, Kindle edition.

They hoped that if they could persist, God would see them through their sorrow and restore Jerusalem.

Job was rich. He was living the blessed life. The Scripture describes him as "blameless and upright" (Job 1:1). God presented him as a standard of integrity to Satan. In response, Satan said that Job only honored God because of all the blessings he received from the Lord. So, in a kind of cosmic wager, God allowed Satan to test Job by stripping him of his possessions, his children, and eventually his health in order to tempt him to renounce God.

But Job refused to sin against God by cursing him. In fact, after raiders and natural disasters took everything from him, still Job said, "The LORD gave, and the LORD has taken away; blessed be the name of the LORD" (1:21). But once Satan took Job's health away too, even his wife questioned why her husband wouldn't give it up. "Do you still hold fast your integrity?" she said. "Curse God and die" (2:9). But Job continued in his faith even in agony.

Perhaps the most trying part of the ordeal for Job was the lack of support from his friends. Although they sat in silence with him for seven days—a welcome display of sympathy—it wasn't long before Eliphaz, Bildad, and Zophar suggested that Job must have been living in sin to have endured such tragedy. As Job defended himself, the suggestions turned into straight-up accusations. Eliphaz, for example, said, "Is not your evil abundant? There is no end to your iniquities. . . . Therefore snares are all around you, and sudden terror overwhelms you" (22:5, 10). So not only was Job the victim of (seemingly) random tragedies, but his own friends blamed him for his misfortune.

Although they were jerks in their delivery, it's hard to fault Job's "friends" for their belief system. Since Eliphaz, Bildad, and Zophar probably lived prior to the Exodus, they would not have had the Proverbs at their disposal. But even though they lived pre-Solomon, these friends were wise men in their own rights,[58] and conventional wisdom from the Ancient Near East agreed with Solomon. You reap what you sow. The diligent prosper. Punishment comes to the wicked. Consider it an ancient sort of karma sans reincarnation. This mindset fueled Job's friends to conclude he had done something to deserve the tragedies that had come his way, and every time Job defended himself and declared his innocence, the bolder and ruder his friends became.

This sort of reap-what-you-sow mentality prevailed in New Testament times and even has a grip on today's culture. Remember what the disciples asked Jesus about the blind man? *Who sinned that he was born blind?* Their underlying premise needs no explanation because we all understand it: if this man did nothing wrong, it would not be fair for him to be blind from birth.

So if there were only one lesson to take from Job, it is that bad things *do* happen to good people. Every day. All the time. Cancer, car wrecks, natural disasters, drive-by shootings, and on and on— these things happen to undeserving people quite often. As true as the wisdom of Proverbs is, sometimes the wise *don't* live long lives. Sometimes they die young. You won't get that lesson unless you read Job.

So living with a Proverbs-only worldview means that when you're in the midst of tragedy, you become disillusioned, and when you're on the outside, you assume the victim is also the criminal. You get preachers proclaiming terrorist attacks are punishment for sin. *Really? You're comfortable speaking for God?* Could such a reality be true? Yes, but likely not. Here's why: these types of catastrophic punishments historically come with prolonged warnings from God's prophets combined with signs and wonders to confirm those warnings. This

---

[58] Ibid, 64129.

discussion merits more than a couple of sentences, but since it's not our primary focus, we'll leave it at that. But I bring this up only to show that when tragedies occur, we always ask why. It is human nature to try to make sense of events, so some invent stories about God's retribution with little more than circumstantial evidence to back them up. Is American culture marching further away from Judeo-Christian morality? Yes, a little more every day, it seems. But the reality is that sometimes terrorist organizations plot to destroy things they don't like. And sometimes they succeed.

Try as we might to find them, good reasons often don't exist for the misfortunes that befall us under the sun. Order and justice do exist, but many times it requires us—just as with blessings—to view them through the lens of eternity.

Your Utmost Is Not Enough

So how can we reconcile the apparent incongruities we see among the wisdom books of the Bible? Proverbs reads as sweet as honey, Ecclesiastes as if you ate an entire jar, and Job like a punch to the gut. Are these just isolated books that contradict one another? If so, which philosophy should we embrace?

Although they're separate books, we should read Proverbs and Ecclesiastes as on a continuum, with Ecclesiastes serving as a sequel of sorts to Proverbs. Doing so helps give us a more complete perspective of knowledge, blessing, and walking in wisdom. When we read these as two clauses joined together, we get something like this for a summary: walking in wisdom *usually* results in a long, happy, and blessed life, but be careful not to put too much stock in worldly knowledge and blessings; they are all meaningless without God in the picture.

The words of wisdom in Proverbs are sound, practical aphorisms that will help us live in peace and achieve prosperity . . . most of the time. We know from the book of Job and from experience that things outside of our control can crash into our lives at any moment. Accidents, illnesses, storms, and more sideswipe the wisest of folks. These people didn't do anything wrong according to wisdom's standards, but due to chance, the corrupted nature of our world, and free will, bad things happen to the undeserving all the time, in every nation, and at all periods throughout history. But just because we can't say that the Proverbs will lead us to desired results 100% of the time does not mean we should rip those pages out of our Bibles. The advice contained in the book *is* wise, and adhering to these aphorisms with Christ at the center of all we do will lead to a good life as far as we have any control in the matter.

But Ecclesiastes can also teach us that we don't often know what is good for us. Were it up to us, we'd all be driving Ferraris and vacationing in exotic locations. But for some, money is a ruiner. Look no further than lottery winners. How many stories have you heard about people who won the lottery only to see their lives unravel before their eyes? Take, for example, the story of David Lee Edwards from Ashland, Kentucky. At the age of forty-six, Edwards and his girlfriend, Shawna Maddux, stopped at a Clark's Pump-N-Shop convenience store to purchase $7 worth of Powerball lottery tickets on their way to the Ashland Plaza Hotel to go drinking.[59] It was a decision he'd probably take back if he could.

Earlier that day, Edwards borrowed money from a friend to have his water turned on again, but he had enough left over for lotto tickets and a night out with Shawna. When officials drew the Powerball numbers, Edwards found himself the winner of a quarter-

---

[59] Kenneth Hart, "Powerball Winner David Lee Edwards Dies at 58 in Ashland," *The Ashland Daily Independent*, December 2, 2013, https://www.kentucky.com/news/state/kentucky/article44456535.html.

share of a $295 million prize. Just about every move he made thereafter was a mistake.

He took the lump sum instead of rationing out his winnings over time, which reduced his earnings from $73.7 to $41 million, which further dwindled to $27 million once Uncle Sam siphoned off his share.[60] Still, plenty of cash for an ex-con, out-of-work Kentuckian and his fiancée, right?

Unable to wait sixteen days for the lump sum payment to arrive, Edwards took out a $200,000 loan so he and Shawna could celebrate in Vegas.[61] Within six days, he had spent every cent of the loan. When the lotto check finally cleared his account, David and Shawna went on a spending bender. They purchased a $1.5 million home in Palm Beach Gardens, Florida. He bought vehicles totaling $1 million. Eventually, he purchased his own jet for $1.9 million. The list of expenditures goes on: jewelry, drugs, vacations, expensive gifts for friends, and a $30,000 TV. He even purchased a $45,000 Hummer golf cart for his eleven-year-old daughter from a previous marriage. Within a year of hitting the lotto, David estimated he'd spent $12 million dollars—almost half of his winnings.

Things spiraled out of control quickly. By mid-2003, Shawna had spent time in multiple rehab facilities because of her drug use, and in 2004, David asked a judge to commit her to a detox clinic again. He said he was afraid she would die from an overdose, having found her passed out with a needle in her arm on multiple occasions.[62] Then, in October 2004, police responded to a domestic violence call at the Edwards' Florida home. Shawna had allegedly stabbed David with her crack pipe and kicked him the chest. He crawled out of the house and shouted for help.

---

[60] Ibid.

[61] Amy Guthrie, "Powerfall," *New Times Broward-Palm Beach*, August 16, 2007, https://www.browardpalmbeach.com/news/powerfall-6343518.

[62] Ibid.

David wasn't drug-free himself. In fact, he and Shawna both contracted hepatitis from using dirty needles to inject themselves with drugs. If things weren't bad enough, child welfare removed David's daughter and Shawna's youngest son from their home due to the unsafe environment the couple had created.

Within five years of winning the Powerball lottery, David Lee Edwards was broke. He lost his home to foreclosure, and he and Shawna moved into a warehouse facility that David rented to store vehicles and other possessions. Not long after moving in, the couple was evicted, and the auctioneer hired to sell the remaining possessions found needles and feces on the ground, despite the fact that the space had a working toilet.[63]

With nothing left, Shawna drove David to an Orlando hospital due to his failing health. The couple divorced in 2008. At fifty-eight, David died penniless in hospice care in 2013.

Was the million-dollar jackpot a blessing to David Lee Edwards of Ashland, Kentucky? Decidedly not. But Edwards thought it was at the time: "The first thing first thing I did was thank God," he said.[64]

Edwards's tale is one of many who squandered their lottery winnings. But lest you think such a story is merely anecdotal, consider this. Research published in *The Review of Economics and Statistics* revealed that Florida residents who win between $50,000 and $150,000 are around six times *more* likely than the average Floridian to file bankruptcy in the three- to five-year period following their win.[65] What we consider a blessing might actually be harmful

---

[63] Ibid.

[64] "From Unemployment to Powerball Millionaire," CNN.com, WarnerMedia, August 27, 2001, http://www.cnn.com/2001/US/08/27/edwards.transcript/.

[65] Scott Hankins, Mark Hoekstra, and Paige Marta Skiba, "The Ticket to

to us. If you have children, you see this almost every day. I don't allow my children to have a third ice cream sandwich—not because I'm a jerk who doesn't want my kids to have tasty treats, but because I don't want them to get sick to their stomachs or have to deal with long-term health issues caused by excessive sweets. This is kind of a ridiculous example, but how many of us ask God for yet another ice cream sandwich? Yes, we have two running cars, clean water, electricity, two well-paying jobs, and a beautiful family. *But God, could you just bless us with a pay raise so we can go to Disney World this summer?*

There's nothing at all wrong with Disney World. I've been many times, and it's quite fun. The problem arises when one treats it like a need or a birthright. A trip to Disney World, as fun as it is, can actually be a curse if you don't have your financial house in order.

Therefore, we must rely on God to provide us with the blessings he knows we need. It's okay to ask God for things, but only if you do so with the right spirit. We must approach the throne with confidence but also with humility in asking for blessings, deferring to God's wisdom in such matters. It's as Jesus prayed, "Not my will, but yours, be done" (Lk. 22:42). In other words, you must be prepared for God to say no and to accept that answer. If you can't do that, don't even ask. Solomon, who was the wisest man ever to have lived, found out that all the wisdom in the world is like a pebble

---

Easy Street? The Financial Consequences of Winning the Lottery," *The Review of Economics and Statistics* 93, no. 3 (2011): 962. The study found that approximately 4.3% of Florida residents who won between $50,000 and $150,000 filed bankruptcy in years 3–5 after winning. Statistics from the American Bankruptcy Institute, coupled with census data, show the bankruptcy rate among Floridian adults to hover around .7%

compared to the mountain of God's knowledge and understanding. He also learned that the things he thought would bring happiness and fulfillment—riches, achievements, palaces, peace, sex, alcohol, fine dining, respect, and even wisdom itself—could not provide any lasting contentment. Attempting to derive fulfillment from anything other than God is futile.

I'd venture to say that one could read Proverbs with secular eyes; obey its maxims encouraging us to be generous, work hard, and seek out knowledge and wisdom; and, as a result, live a prosperous life. But even so, one thing would be true: it wouldn't be fulfilling. One interesting fact about Proverbs is that the wisdom tradition did not originate with Solomon or with the Israelites. Excavations throughout the ancient world have uncovered tablets containing aphorisms from Egypt, Ebla (Syria), and Mesopotamia predating the kingdom of Israel.[66] Therefore, it is quite probable that Solomon borrowed from the wisdom literature of other cultures. As he himself taught, part of being wise is seeking out the wisdom of others. In accessing this global knowledge, Solomon recited things he found out through his God-given discernment and experience to be true. But notice the twist he adds near the beginning of Proverbs: "The fear of the LORD is the beginning of knowledge; fools despise wisdom and instruction" (1:7). This slant is unique to Israel's wisdom literature. True wisdom, Solomon says, must first come from a healthy relationship with God. And whatever we say about the incongruity between Proverbs and Ecclesiastes, they do agree on this point. Here's Solomon's conclusion to the latter book: "The end of the matter; all has been heard. Fear God and keep his commandments, for this is the whole duty of man. For God will bring every deed into judgment,

---

[66] Bruce K. Waltke, "The Book of Proverbs and Ancient Wisdom Literature," *Bibliotheca Sacra* 136, July-September (1979): 222-223.

with every secret thing, whether good or evil" (12:13–14).

With some reconciliation between these two books, let's revisit Job briefly. He did everything right and still endured sorrow, pain, and loss. He feared God. He was a man of integrity. But he lost it all. Not because he was unwise or rash or because he sinned, but because God was testing him. We will talk much more about loss and the why behind the evils we see all around us in part three, but for now, here's one last takeaway from Job in light of Proverbs.

You can do everything right and still lose it all.

So how, then, should we approach life? As one waiting for tragedy? Should we become nihilists or pessimists and burn Solomon's advice? By no means. We *should* read and follow the advice of Proverbs, understanding that doing so will often lead to peace, prosperity, and esteem. But we should not be so naive to think that doing so forces God's hand or that our lives will be free from misfortune. That's insane.

You may be familiar with the daily devotional known as *My Utmost for His Highest*. The devotional is a collection of sermons and lectures from Oswald Chambers, who lived a remarkable life of service to God. The Scot spent time in Japan as a missionary, opened a school in England, and worked for the YMCA as a chaplain in Egypt during World War I. In 1917, at just forty-three, Chambers died from complications of appendicitis. In his absence, Biddy, his widow, self-published the collection of Oswald's writings that she herself had compiled over the years.[67]

The titular phrase comes from the January 1 entry, in which Oswald reflects on Philippians 1:20. Chambers argues that Jesus is asking us to yield to him in certain areas of our lives, but often we

---

[67] "Oswald Chambers' Bio," My Utmost for His Highest, https://utmost.org/oswald-chambers-bio.

hesitate to obey for any number of reasons. Paraphrasing Paul's words, Chambers writes, "'My determination is to be my utmost for His Highest.' To get there is a question of the will . . . an absolute and irrevocable surrender on that point."[68]

I agree wholeheartedly with this philosophy: that we should give our all for the glory of God. Please don't think that I don't. But as a perfection addict, I've had to learn this lesson the hard way: your utmost is not enough. Scripture describes Job as "blameless and upright," and yet he lost everything.[69] You can give it your utmost and still have everything come crashing down around you. From an eternal perspective, your utmost is not enough either. We can never be good enough or holy enough to earn admittance to heaven. Instead, we rely on the grace God pours out on those who would receive it.

Of course, Chambers wasn't claiming that we should give our utmost for our own gain, but rather "for His highest." Approaching life with this motive shifts the focus away from ourselves and onto our creator—just the way it should be. And although it is not enough, all God wants is your utmost. As the greatest commandment teaches us, "Love the LORD your God with all your heart and with all your soul and with all your might" (Deut. 6:5). God honors and, yes, blesses those who give their best to him, even though such rewards might not happen this side of eternity.

Knowing as much still doesn't make pain and sorrow easy to bear. But proper context and motive can often provide meaning in difficult times and make things a little less burdensome.

---

[68] Oswald Chambers, *My Utmost for His Highest* (Uhrichsville, OH: Barbour, 1963), January 1st entry.
[69] See Job 1:8.

Part III

When Bad Things Do Happen

CHAPTER 8
The Curious Case of the Suffering Christian

The longer we spend in eternity, the more the sufferings of this life will shrink by comparison toward an infinitesimal moment.
—Dr. William Lane Craig[70]

Freedom and the fall explain suffering, but that doesn't make evil easy to bear.

Answering why is often half the battle. We resist meaninglessness because we understand intuitively that life has meaning. We've touched on the why of suffering at times throughout this book, but let's dive a bit deeper here.

Answering this question will, no doubt, open up a can of theological worms for some folks, so I promise to try my best to recapture each little night crawler and stick them back in the can before screwing the lid on. Nevertheless, despite our best efforts, it's likely a few might get away.

---

[70] William Lane Craig, *On Guard: Defending Your Faith with Reason and Precision* (Colorado Springs, CO: David C. Cook, 2010), Kindle edition, 167.

Why Evil?

As I see it, two sources of suffering exist: evil (i.e. intentional, purposeful suffering inflicted on another) and amoral suffering. Amoral suffering is random, unintentional, and accidental. This can range anywhere from a stubbed toe to a tsunami. We'll deal with evil first.

To say that evil exists is actually a religious statement. You might think such an assertion—that evil exists—is obvious and needs no explanation or defense. Just look at Hitler, Stalin, or the Oakland Raiders, and it's quite apparent that dark forces are at play. British journalist Malcolm Muggeridge agreed, writing, "The depravity of the human heart is at once the most intellectually resisted yet most empirically verifiable reality."[71] Nevertheless, the assertion of evil is an admission of good. How can one exist without the other? To say that an act is evil implies that there is a way things ought to be (goodness), but such a behavior failed to live up to the standards of goodness (evil). Again, not exactly a controversial statement, but in the random, amoral, programmatic world of naturalism, nothing can truly be good or evil. All matter is simply atoms floating around in space, all emotions just chemical reactions in the brain.

This fact is important to establish: we cannot question the presence of evil without asserting the existence of some sort of standard of goodness. Following this line of thinking eventually leads one to God. But this, then, opens the doors wide for our question at hand: *Why? How can a good God allow evil to persist?*

The simple answer is that God grants humans free will. He created us in his image, part of which results in freedom of choice.

---

[71] As quoted in Ravi Zacharias, *The End of Reason: A Response to the New Atheists* (Grand Rapids, MI: Zondervan, 2008), Kindle edition, location 670 of 1528.

We have some agency over our lives. God gives us the ability to reason and understand abstract concepts. Animals, in contrast, just act on instinct. If carnivores kill other animals, can they be held accountable? Of course not. They acted based on predetermined genetic programming. Some mother rabbits will eat their newborn babies. Should we lock them up or euthanize them for their crimes? No. They know not what they do. Humans, of course, *do* know what they do, and we often choose the wrong thing.

Of course, to ascribe evil to humanity requires a few underlying premises to be true, all of which I think you'll agree with, as they are not controversial. We've already discussed the first: evil exists. If evil does not exist, then the question self-destructs.

The second assumption is that God is always benevolent. The Scriptures teach us in numerous passages that this is true, so it's up to you whether or not to believe them. The psalmist wrote, "Taste and see that the LORD is good!" (34:8). And Jesus himself said, "No one is good except God alone" (Mk. 10:18). This assumption is required because if God is not all good all the time, then we could easily write off evil as the whims of a capricious god. Nevertheless, God, by definition, is good. Were he not, he would cease to be God.

The third assumption is that God is all-powerful. Just as with benevolence, omnipotence is an essential characteristic of God. Paul wrote of God's "eternal power and divine nature" (Rom. 1:20). Jesus said, "Nothing will be impossible with God" (Lk. 1:37). Those who do not operate under this assumption could conclude that there are forces of evil too strong for God to contend with. For the creator of the universe, such a proposition is ridiculous, akin to asking, "Could God create a rock too heavy for him to lift?" The question is self-defeating and doesn't follow the rules of logic because it assumes that God operates in the same realm as his creation, with the limitations of gravity and even matter itself. Similarly, to assume some force of evil exists that is too powerful for God is a ridiculous proposition when you follow the thread logically. Any force or presence in existence springs from the creator. God, in fact, is the only being in existence who has no cause, no starting point. He is infinite, meaning he will not only exist forever, but has always existed. God has no starting point.

But if all forces have a cause and God is the cause of all things, doesn't that mean he caused evil? And, if so, doesn't this shatter our second assumption that God is good? Here's where the three assumptions coalesce and the concept of free will emerges.

Why Did God Create Humanity?

Have you ever pondered this question? If not, your gut reaction might be to say that God created humans because he was lonely. But this answer comes from our human perspective. Just so there's no ambiguity: God was not lonely. The Father, Son, and Holy Spirit existed in a loving, triune relationship prior to creation. These three persons in one God have always existed. For evidence, look at the creation narrative, in which God says, "Let *us* make man in our image, after our likeness" (Gen. 1:26, emphasis added). God used the first person plural to reference the Trinity.

So if God was not lonely, why create humans? He created us to share his love with us. His desire is that we might enter into a loving relationship with him. But introducing that word, *love*, immediately creates a problem. In order for one to love, he or she must have the ability to *choose* to love. If one is forced or programmed to loved, is such a result really love? No; rather, it is manipulation. True love can only result from two persons freely choosing one another.

But the ability to choose introduces a problem for non-gods. For imperfect beings to have choices, we must have the ability to choose the wrong thing.[72] And, inevitably, we all do. Just as Paul wrote to the Romans, "All have sinned and fall short of the glory of God" (3:23). Therefore, this first type of suffering we experience, evil, is a direct result of sin. Every sin we commit has consequences. Sin establishes a barrier between God and us, causes us pain, and inflicts pain on others. Sin nailed Jesus to a cross. Much of the suffering we see and experience in the world today can be explained by the choices we make. When Adam and Eve ate the forbidden fruit, Adam had to deal with thorns and thistles, and Eve had to contend with birth pains. From grandiose acts like the September 11 attacks down to small-scale acts like one coworker slandering another, people choose to inflict harm on others and themselves every day.

So why choose to create us at all if God knew such suffering would exist? This, obviously, is a lengthy philosophical discussion, but the short answer is that the glory of the end result supersedes the suffering in the interim. (We'll discuss this more below.)

Who Sinned?

The second kind of suffering we experience is of the incidental, unintentional type. These are things like natural disasters, cancer, car accidents, and the like. In these cases, the cause of pain is not a direct result of sin, but rather an effect of nature's cruelty or the randomness of chance. I say "not a direct result" because sin still is the root cause.

---

[72] I must make it clear that I don't believe that humans have unlimited free will. My children have free will, but being larger and stronger than they are, I snatch them up out of the street if they meander into traffic. They do not choose to be saved from a collision, but I save them nevertheless. Furthermore, the existence of free will does nothing to limit God's sovereignty, as some claim. We only have any choice at all because God grants it to us—and, being omnipotent, he could revoke that freedom at any time if he so desired.

Let's return to Eden for a closer look. Prior to sin, God's creation was perfect. He set up the man and woman in the garden, where they would not die. Have you ever pondered the implications of Adam and Eve's immortality? They were free to eat of any tree but one, yet they did not *have* to eat at all because they could not die. Food was for pleasure only. They couldn't develop cancer, heart disease, or even a cold. The garden was a haven in which no corruption existed. In light of such privilege, the eating of the fruit of the tree of the knowledge of good and evil is even more tragic. With a couple of bites, Adam and Eve ushered in an age of corruption and destruction.

Remember our talk about the laws of thermodynamics? It would be wrong to suggest that these laws didn't apply prior to the fall of mankind. After all, tasks as simple as walking would be nearly impossible without friction. The act of pushing off the ground with the foot transfers energy from the body to the ground. Try walking without friction. It would be a bit like running on an iced-over pond with banana peel shoes. Nevertheless, there are some elements to thermodynamics that God overruled prior to sin. The key concept to keep in mind is that the laws of thermodynamics explain what happens in a closed system. But remember, God exists outside of this system. He operates in a different realm than his creation. God was present in Eden and was a source of infinite energy. As a result, there was no decay or corruption in the garden like we see in the laws of thermodynamics.

But when Adam and Eve disobeyed God, their first sin was the first step in the march toward the heat death of the universe. Our God is a God of order, but the second law teaches that entropy (a measure of disorder) is always increasing. God, of course, is able to restore order, but sin separates us from him. Just look at the consequences for the first sins:

To the woman he said,
  "I will surely multiply your pain in childbearing;
  in pain you shall bring forth children.
  Your desire shall be contrary to your husband,
  but he shall rule over you."
And to Adam he said,
  "Because you have listened to the voice of your wife
  and have eaten of the tree
  of which I commanded you,
  'You shall not eat of it,'
  cursed is the ground because of you;
  in pain you shall eat of it all the days of your life;
  thorns and thistles it shall bring forth for you;
  and you shall eat the plants of the field.
  By the sweat of your face
  you shall eat bread,
  till you return to the ground,
  for out of it you were taken;
  for you are dust,
  and to dust you shall return."
Genesis 3:16–19

To bring forth new life now required pain and effort. "By the sweat" of Adam's face he would eat bread. Now it requires effort to procure food, burning calories to get calories. Thorns and thistles get in our way and creation turns on itself: predator on prey, brother against brother, hailstorms on crops. As a direct result of Adam and Eve's sin, creation was plunged into corruption. Everything is in a state of decay and decline. Did you know that the earth's rotation is slowing down slightly every day? Did you know that the sun will eventually burn out? These are all direct results of the introduction of sin—the antithesis of God—into his perfect creation.

These consequences were devastating to Adam and Eve, but even worse was their ouster from God's presence. They were isolated from him, his love, and his restorative, sustaining qualities. Interestingly, we see a reversal of the second law of thermodynamics in the book of Revelation:

> *No longer will there be anything accursed, but the throne of God and of the Lamb will be in it, and his servants will worship him. . . . And night will be no more. They will need no light of lamp or sun, for the Lord God will be their light, and they will reign forever and ever.*
> Revelation 22:3, 5

This passage describes what the New Jerusalem will look like after God deals with evil once and for all. When before we were headed to a terrifying notion of a universal heat death, here God becomes the infinite source of energy. Of course, God has always been the source of all energy, matter, and life, but prior to sin, creation was in union with God. Sin, by necessity, separates us from him. Therefore, we have heart attacks, tornadoes, and hurricanes. (Of course, eating too much bacon can cause heart disease too, but no matter how well someone treats his body, it will eventually break down.) Some people who are way smarter than I am argue that natural disasters would continue to occur regardless of the fall; it's just that God isolated and protected Adam and Eve from them. Author Paul Copan, for example, argues that natural evils are necessary to providing livable conditions. He writes:

> *As surprising as it may seem, events such as hurricanes, tornadoes, or earthquakes are actually necessary for the benefit of humankind. Planetary scientists affirm that these*

events must *occur for the earth to maintain its delicate balances of atmospheric and other environmental conditions necessary for humans to survive. . . [for example] The shifting of tectonic plates (which results in earthquakes) allows the essential nutrients for life to be recycled back onto the continents.*[73]

I disagree with Copan here. Although I'm sure the science checks out, God could maintain livable conditions on earth by any means he chooses. Many realities we know about, such as the laws of thermodynamics, were in play in Eden, but it is irrefutable that some fundamental things changed with the fall. It is impossible for a human to live forever, and yet that was God's promise to the first humans as long as they did not eat the forbidden fruit. So if something as extreme as eternal life could be accomplished, is it really a stretch to think that God could recycle carbon dioxide back into the air without hurricanes or replenish essential minerals without invoking earthquakes? To the naturalist, this is, of course, unfathomable, but then again, so is the notion of God. Yet to the Christian, sustainable life without devastation is not unimaginable at all.

Regardless of the pre-fall reality, the truth of the matter is that Adam and Eve could not die. Therefore, even had natural disasters occurred, God would have shielded them from their devastating effects. They would not have had heart attacks no matter how much ice cream they ate. Sin is the ultimate corrupter of everything, including the Earth. So to go back to our example of the blind man in John 9, the disciples assumed that the man or his parents had sinned, which caused him to be born without sight. They assumed this because that was the only

---

[73] Paul Copan, *That's Just Your Interpretation: Responding to Skeptics Who Challenge Your Faith* (Grand Rapids, MI: Baker Books, 2001), Kindle Edition, 97.

explanation they could muster for the man's impairment. But Jesus affirmed, "It was not that this man sinned, or his parents, but that the works of God might be displayed in him" (v. 3). And yet, while sin was not the direct cause of the man's blindness, the fall of mankind indirectly led to disabilities, defects, accidents, and natural disasters. So, taking the disciples' question more broadly, "Who sinned?" we might answer with sincerity, "We all did."

What to Do If You Struggle with Loss

Understanding suffering and the causes of evil on an intellectual level often does little good for those swept up in the throes of tragedy. It is, as philosophy professor Daniel Howard-Snyder wrote, a bit like offering someone "a cold stone when only warm bread will do."[74] This is not to say that stones are not useful. In fact, bread, while nourishing, will only last someone for a day. But one can use stone to build a solid foundation that could last centuries. But Abraham Maslow reminds us that until the basics like food and shelter and met, no one possesses the bandwidth to concern themselves with complex building projects. Therefore, we must take some time to address the hunger created by loss. What do we do when we struggle with loss?

Refuse to Blame God

Perhaps we should start with what not to do: blame God. I know it's tempting, but he's not the source of your pain. And even if he were the source, it would be only to achieve some sort of greater good at

---

[74] Daniel Howard-Snyder, Michael J. Murray, ed., *Reason for the Hope Within* (Grand Rapids, MI: William B. Eerdmans Publishing Company, 1999), 80.

which you could not otherwise arrive. But couldn't he have prevented the tragedy? Yes, but as we saw previously, God has granted humanity free will, which inevitably leads to all sorts of evils. Why create this type of reality at all, knowing how much suffering would come about? The answer to this question is key. The only possible explanation for a benevolent, omniscient, omnipotent god to create a world with so much suffering is if he knew the end result would be worth it and if there were no other way.

Think about that for a moment. Let your mind go to the most horrific evil you can fathom. The glory and goodness which will arise from such hideousness will far surpass the suffering we see and experience around us. In fact, it will be so glorious that our finite minds cannot even comprehend it.

Job is our shining example here. He lost his children, lost all his wealth, and developed agonizing sores all over his body. If anyone had a reason to blame God, it was Job. Remember what Job's own wife said to him? "Do you still hold fast your integrity? Curse God and die" (Job 2:9). But Job, despite these terrible circumstances, said something insightful: "You speak as one of the foolish women would speak. Shall we receive good from God, and shall we not receive evil?" (v. 10). In other words, are you only going to stick with God when times are good? If you've ever been to a wedding or watched any romantic comedy films lately, you've probably heard vows the man and woman take, agreeing to stay together "in sickness and in health, for richer or for poorer." I myself said similar words, but I assure you that on my wedding day, I had no grasp of the weight those words carry. My image of marriage was one of eternal bliss where the bed was always made, money flowed like water, and neither of us ever got sick. I suspect for many newlyweds, the expectation is the same.

Many people also come to Christ under the same pretenses. *My life will be perfect all the time*, the thinking goes. The reality, though, is far from it. The old G. K. Chesterton quotation always comes to my mind in these situations: "When belief in God becomes difficult, the tendency is to turn away from Him; but in heaven's name to what?"[75] Where else could we go for solace or comfort or restoration? No one but God can offer what we need. It's okay—and quite natural—to feel hurt by God, and to ask why, but doing so with anger or in an accusatory way (though, again, quite natural) is counterproductive. Be honest with God and cling to him. Tell him you're confused and sad. Ask him why. Job did: "Why have you made me your mark? Why have I become a burden to you?" (7:20). But for heaven's sake, don't turn away from the one who has all of the answers. This leads us to the next point.

Continue in Your Spiritual Disciplines

Remember those habits you developed in chapter two? Hold on to them. Prioritize reading the Word, praying, and attending church. Lean in to the fellowship of believers around you. No matter how boring, difficult, or horrible reading the Scriptures seems at these moments in your life, keep it up. Make a commitment to read and pray to God every day, even if you just slog through it. Some days will seem like a waste, but keeping up the habit will yield breakthrough days in which you experience God like never before.

Your quiet time with God is one of those keystone habits that forms a foundation for your day-to-day living and your life as a whole. The book of Hebrews teaches that "the word of God is living and active, sharper than any two-edged sword, piercing to the division of soul and of spirit, of joints and of marrow, and discerning

---

[75] G. K. Chesterton, as quoted in Ravi Zacharias, *Cries of the Heart: Bringing God Near When He Feels So Far* (Nashville: Thomas Nelson, 2002), 65.

the thoughts and intentions of the heart" (4:12). God's revelation to us isn't a passive, dusty book on a shelf; it actively reveals our own hearts to us. When we're thrust into the throes of unfair tragedies, our stubborn refusal to turn away from God will yield discernment and spiritual growth.

Another critical component is maintaining connection with the body of Christ. If you aren't part of a church, you need to find one now. Fellow believers can lift you up while you mourn. For some, this advice is obvious. But for others, it probably seems painful. I get it. I'm an introvert, and I also hate asking other people for anything. Nevertheless, the church can be a source of great encouragement to you when you are in need. Let's return to Hebrews for a moment; the author writes, "Let us consider how to stir up one another to love and good works, not neglecting to meet together, as is the habit of some, but encouraging one another, and all the more as you see the Day drawing near" (10:24–25). We can look at this passage two ways. The first is that those who forsake fellowship with other believers miss out on the encouragement that the body of Christ can provide. The second is this: it is wrong to skip gatherings because you miss out on the opportunity to encourage others. It is the responsibility of church members to lift each other up in love.

In 1 Corinthians, Paul refers to the church using the analogy of a body. He writes, "For just as the body is one and has many members, and all the members of the body, though many, are one body, so it is with Christ. For in one Spirit we were all baptized into one body" (12:12–13). No doubt you have at some point suffered an injury to a specific part of your body. When that happens, how do you react? Physiologically, your body registers the pain in such a way that you can think of little else. You do whatever you can to make that part well, whether by creams, stitches, ice, or antibiotics. On the biological scale, your body works to heal the wound. Increased blood flow to the wound helps to carry blood cells to fight any infections. Coagulants form scabs to close the wound as the body works to repair the skin.

In the same way, the church serves as a healing agent to its members. It provides hope, support, and encouragement to those who need it. But for the disembodied member? There is little relief. I know you may be thinking that many churches, or maybe even your church in particular, are not good at caring for its people. Of course, we can always find examples that don't fit the rule, but if your church cannot encourage members, maybe the culture is toxic to the point that you need to leave. Just don't make the decision lightly, as the carpet is not always greener in the other sanctuary.

One Reason for Encouragement in Dark Times

It would be a grave error to start reading the book of Job, but neglect to finish the book. We touched on this already, but the last chapter is the most critical. In the end, what happens? God restores Job. He doubles his fortune, he blesses him with more children, and Job lives a long, happy life. This passage is critical because it demonstrates the divine, omnipotent power of God to set things right. To our modern sensibilities, this last chapter might sound too neat. It might seem like some sort of *deus ex machina*—an unrealistic ending to the story.

Deus ex machina is a literary device storytellers use to solve seemingly unsolvable problems. The term, translated as "god from the machine," originated in ancient Greek dramas in which one of their gods would appear from above to rescue the protagonist from his plight. To make the actor descend from above the scene, stagehands would use a *mēchanē*—a Greek word for crane.[76] One of the most famous examples of *deus ex machina* is *The Wizard of Oz*, in which Dorothy, apparently trapped in the Land of Oz after the wizard accidentally floats away in his hot air balloon without her, awakens to find herself back in Kansas after a click of her heels. Whether the viewer believes that Oz was merely a dream or not is immaterial; that Dorothy could return home by a click and recitation of "There's no place like home" is the real *deus ex machina*—an unexplained, magical resolution to an impossible problem.

Although these endings can be cheesy or unsatisfying, viewers and readers of stories involving this plot resolution tool generally accept them, having already suspended their disbelief for the duration of the film. (Flying monkeys? Anthropomorphic scarecrows? Really?) Therefore, for ruby slippers to be the answer to the protagonist's plight is not a problem. But when it comes to real life? Those kinds of things simply don't happen.

So we read Job with a set of eyes preternaturally set to suspend disbelief and can therefore accept that God restored Job's wealth and health. But when it comes to *my* job loss, *my* physical ailment, or *my* loss of a loved one, such a thing could never occur. Right?

Why Did Jesus Weep?

One of the most moving stories in all of Scripture is that of Jesus's friend Lazarus. Lazarus lived in Bethany, a town just outside of Jerusalem, and he and his sisters opened their home to the Lord whenever he traveled south to the city of David. Once, while Jesus was ministering in Bethabara, Lazarus fell ill. Bethabara, also known

---

[76] *Encyclopaedia Britannica*, s.v. "Deus Ex Machina," last modified March 20, 2020, https://www.britannica.com/art/deus-ex-machina.

as Bethany, was about thirty miles east of Bethany near Jerusalem.[77] Jesus had just been in Judea, but left after some Jews tried to stone him for a second time.[78] This is why, on receiving the message Lazarus was ill, Jesus said, "Let us go to Judea again" (Jn. 11:7).

If you follow the narrative from John chapters 7 through 10, it appears that Jesus came to Jerusalem for the Feast of Booths (also called the Feast of Tabernacles or Sukkot) and spent two to three months in the region teaching. Booths occurs between late September and late October, and John 10 tells us that Jesus taught in Jerusalem at the Feast of Dedication, more commonly known to us as Hanukkah. As you probably know, the Jewish people celebrate Hanukkah in mid to late December. Therefore, Jesus likely spent the majority of autumn in Judea. Because Bethany seems to have been Jesus's southern base, it is not unlikely that he would have spent a considerable amount of time with Lazarus and his two sisters during these months.

So despite the protestations of Thomas, who feared for his life, Jesus and the disciples recrossed the Jordan and headed back to Judea . . . but not right away. Jesus waited two days before leaving one Bethany for the next. Why? It's not because Jesus was cold-hearted. In fact, other than the Twelve, Lazarus was probably Jesus's best friend. For evidence, look no further than the extreme display of emotion from our Savior at Lazarus's tomb. Once there, Jesus burst into tears. And this, despite the knowledge that he would raise him from the dead in a few moments.

Don't miss this point. Jesus (and, by extension, the Father) hurts when we hurt. He loves us so much that our pain and suffering affect him in profound ways. Even though he can (and will) restore order

---

[77] Albert Barnes, *John*, Barnes' Notes on the Bible (1834), John 11:6, https://biblehub.com/commentaries/barnes/john/11.htm.
[78] John 10:31.

and goodness, in the moment—inescapable for mortals, but outside of the scope of a timeless deity—God suffers with us.

In reality, we don't know exactly why Jesus delayed in returning, but perhaps he knew it would not matter. John 11:17 tells us that Lazarus had been in the tomb for four days. That means that by the time word got to Jesus about his friend's condition, Lazarus was already within moments of death, if not already dead. The trip from Bethany to the Bethany beyond the Jordan was about thirty miles of steep terrain—at least one full day's journey. Add the two days Jesus tarried and the full day's trip back to Martha and Mary, and you get four full days, the same time Lazarus spent in the tomb. In other words, Jesus could have left immediately upon receiving news of his friend's illness and Lazarus still would have been dead for two days.

Nevertheless, Scripture does provide some hints for Jesus's delay. He said to his disciples, "Lazarus has died, and for your sake I am glad that I was not there, so that you may believe" (11:14–15). And at the tomb, Jesus said, "Father, I thank you that you have heard me. I knew that you always hear me, but I said this on account of the people standing around, that they may believe that you sent me" (vv. 41–42). In both statements, Jesus said that his desire was that those around him would believe that he was the Messiah, sent by God. Although Jesus didn't cause the tragedy (original sin is the root cause of death), he used it to bring about belief in him—a belief that leads to life everlasting.

This is how God operates. He takes what is nasty, rotten, corrupt, and heartbreaking and flips it for good. As the source of life and all things good, he can use any situation or tragedy to bring about redemption—even the death of a loved one.

Upon Jesus's arrival in Bethany, Martha came to him, and the two engaged in one of the most poignant conversations in Scripture. Martha protests that had Jesus been there, he could have saved her brother. Jesus replied, "Your brother will rise again." Martha said to him, "I know that he will rise again in the resurrection on the last day" (vv. 23–24).

Martha was hoping for more, but she took solace in the fact that God would resurrect her brother at the end of days. Then Jesus responded, "I am the resurrection and the life. Whoever believes in me, though he die, yet shall he live, and everyone who lives and believes in me shall never die. Do you believe this?" (vv. 25–26). Martha did believe.

Jesus *is* the resurrection and the life. He is the embodiment of vitality, the essence of being. As the Scripture teaches, "In him we live and move and have our being" (Acts 17:28). For those who believe in him, death is but a pause, a comma in the book of our lives. When everything seems dark, when life seems hopeless, Jesus is there to offer grace where it is not deserved and restoration to the corruption of this world. He is the antidote to the unpleasant consequences of thermodynamics—an infinite source of energy in a world that is burning itself out. *How is this possible?* You might ask. Unlike with Greek gods and other authorial contrivances, Jesus is *Deus extra machina*—the God who exists *outside* of the machine. He transcends this world and its limitations because he created it. The question Jesus is asking you is the same question he asked Martha: "Do you believe this?"

You know the rest of the story. Jesus visited the tomb, wept, prayed to God, and then raised his friend from the dead—his most impressive miracle to date.

So am I saying that if you lost a daughter or an aunt or a brother that God will raise him or her from the dead? No, probably not in this life, but that doesn't mean it is impossible.[79] As an omnipotent

---

[79] There are multiple good apologetic answers for why miracles, though they still occur, are not as overt or frequent as they were in certain biblical epochs. This discussion is somewhat outside the scope of this book, but I'd recommend taking a gander at chapter 8, "Miracles: Signs of God or

being, God is capable of restoring anything in an instant. Unlike good witches from the North or Greek deities, our God is the true *Deus*. And just because restoration may not happen in the here and now does not mean God is incapable or callous. Instead, he has his own reasons for delay, just as Jesus waited two days at Bethabara.

In these moments of heartache, we would do well to remember Romans 8, in which Paul offers comfort to those living in dark times. You should take some time to read the entire chapter, but here are the highlights for brevity's sake:

> *I consider that the sufferings of this present time are not worth comparing with the glory that is to be revealed to us. For the creation waits with eager longing for the revealing of the sons of God. For the creation was subjected to futility, not willingly, but because of him who subjected it, in hope that the creation itself will be set free from its bondage to corruption and obtain the freedom of the glory of the children of God. For we know that the whole creation has been groaning together in the pains of childbirth until now. And not only the creation, but we ourselves, who have the firstfruits of the Spirit, groan inwardly as we wait eagerly for adoption as sons, the redemption of our bodies. For in this hope we were saved. . . . And we know that for those who love God all things work together for good, for those who are called according to his purpose.*
> Romans 8:18–24, 28

Whatever you're going through, no matter how painful or unjust, is infinitesimal compared to the glory that is to come. God as creator

---

Gullibility?", in Norman Geisler and Frank Turek's book *I Don't Have Enough Faith to Be an Atheist* (Wheaton, IL: Crossway, 2004).

and sustainer of life is able to restore everything we lose, whether it's in this life or the next. And that restoration will be so complete, so awesome and overwhelming, there will be no trace of heartache. So while we all groan inwardly at the bastardization that sin has brought to God's beautiful creation, take heart that God, in his own time and in his own way, will make everything whole again. It is as Paul wrote: "All things work together for good, for those who are called according to his purpose" (Rom. 8:28). Or again, as Jesus said, "Whoever believes in me, though he die, yet shall he live, and everyone who lives and believes in me shall never die" (Jn. 11:25–26).

We don't always know why awful things happen or why God allows them to persist, but we can rest assured that as a benevolent being, he has our best interests at heart. As we endure hardship, we can look forward to the fulfillment of Revelation 21:4, on the last day, when God will "wipe away every tear . . . and death shall be no more, neither shall there be mourning, nor crying, nor pain anymore, for the former things have passed away." So when you must endure dark times, be encouraged by this fact: God will restore all things.

Dear Person in Pain: God Sees Your Tears

I'm not the greatest at making new friends. I won't engage in psychoanalysis because that would be both boring and self-defeating. But when my family moved from Kansas to northern Nevada when I was twelve, I was excited at first. We all were. It was a new journey—moving to an unknown land to seek adventure and prosperity. We were kind of like the Donner party minus all of the death, starvation, and cannibalism.

When we moved, I didn't know that I wasn't great at making new friends. We had lived in the same house for almost as long as I could remember—a good seven years—so I was always around the same people at school and church. Within a few months of moving, the loneliness set in. I was in a new school as a seventh grader, new state, new everything. I didn't know anyone. I remember once my mom encouraged me to seek out friends, and I just lay on the floor in despair. I started to cry. She might as well have told me to discover cold fusion or speak Mandarin. I didn't even know where to begin.

How to Deal with the Loneliness of Anguish

When King Hezekiah heard from Isaiah that he was going to die, he waited. He waited for the prophet to leave his chambers. He waited until he was alone. Then he did the only reasonable thing: he bawled like a baby and prayed to God. In his desperation, the king prayed, "Now, O LORD, please remember how I have walked before you in faithfulness and with a whole heart, and have done what is good in your sight" (2 Kgs. 20:3).

Though he didn't say it (and maybe I'm reading too much into the Scripture), you can almost hear Hezekiah saying, "Why me? I've been faithful and good, unlike my dad, Ahaz, who burned his own son, my brother, as a sacrifice to a false god. Why me?" That moment must have been the loneliest of Hezekiah's life. And yet, before Isaiah could even leave the palace, God called him back. He said to Isaiah, "Turn back, and say to Hezekiah the leader of my people, Thus says the LORD, the God of David your father: I have heard your prayer; I have seen your tears. Behold, I will heal you" (v. 5).

I wish Isaiah would have come and spoken to me that day on the floor and told me the same thing: "I have seen your tears." Isn't that what we all want to hear when we suffer?

I think pain is one of the most isolating experiences one can undergo. Suffering feels so lonely because we can't really share it with anyone. As I write this, Katie is struggling with some kind of cold or virus or something, and even though I've experienced the same symptoms she has hundreds of times before, she can't share them with me. I can't take them from her to lighten her load for a while. Thus, she suffers alone as her body fights off the illness.

So for the king to hear the words "I have seen your tears" must have been even more comforting than the phrase "I will heal you." Don't believe me? Look at Hezekiah's prayer again. He didn't explicitly ask for healing. He asked that God "remember how I have walked before you in faithfulness." In that moment of suffering, Hezekiah felt abandoned, alone. That's why God said he had seen the king's tears. He wanted the king to know that, even though he was in aguish, God was present in the situation.

And though I didn't hear those words, God saw my tears too. It wasn't but a few weeks later that I developed a strong friendship with a boy who came to my dad's new church plant, and we were good friends for the duration of the five years I spent in Nevada.

When you feel alone, when you suffer, know that God is with you. He sees every tear you shed. He knows your pain. He knows every stress and every disappointment you encounter.

CHAPTER 9
Deus intra Machina

You can't have a resurrection without a death.
—Frank Viola[80]

Jesus knows a thing or two about suffering.

As the creator of our universe, it is no big deal for God to restore material things. For the Israelites in the wilderness, he supplied bread out of thin air in the form of manna. He provided water from a rock so they could drink. He restored Job's fortune and health at the conclusion of the man's trials. And God even restored Lazarus's life even though he was dead for four days.

Nevertheless, for God to restore humanity from the curse of our sins, something radical had to occur. You see, sin, no matter how innocent it may seem, must have a consequence. The most extreme of these consequences, as God warned the first couple, is death. This isn't some kind of power play or overreaction to eating a piece of fruit, although such a result is certainly the right of an omnipotent, omniscient God. Instead, death is a natural consequence of sin. All

---

[80] Frank Viola, *God's Favorite Place on Earth* (Colorado Springs, CO: David C Cook, 2013), Kindle edition, 69.

sin results in death. How so?

We know from 1 John that "God is light, and in him is no darkness at all" (1:5). Therefore, sin is the antithesis of God. The two cannot coexist. As a result, sin separates one from God, but therein lies the problem. God is also the source and sustainer of life. Therefore, to be separate from him is to be separate from life. So what's the solution? We must remove the sin on our account in order to be restored to right standing with God.

The problem, of course, is that we cannot accomplish this on our own. Seems like an impossible situation, doesn't it? Were this a novel or a play, this is where the author, out of ideas, would insert some sort of *deus ex machina* to get us out of our predicament. Instead, we get something even more incredible: *deus intra machina*. Let me explain.

Why Send a Messiah?

At the dawn of the first century AD, Israel was looking for restoration too. Having returned from Babylonian exile in the sixth century BC, the Judeans finished rebuilding the Temple around the year 515 BC. Then, under the leadership of Nehemiah, they rebuilt the wall surrounding the city some seventy years later in the mid-fifth century BC.[81] The Jewish people in Jerusalem now had a new Temple and a wall surrounding the city once again, but they still lived under Persian rule at the conclusion of the Old Testament.

When the New Testament opens up four hundred years later, Israel was still a vassal state, but this time to the dominant Roman Empire. In between these eras, Alexander the Great and the Greeks

---

[81] *Encyclopaedia Britannica*, s.v. "Nehemiah," last modified December 8, 2017, https://www.britannica.com/biography/Nehemiah.

conquered the Persians and much of the surrounding areas. Alexander died an untimely death at the age of thirty-two without a will or an heir of ruling age. (His infant child and the child's mother were murdered soon after his death.) Therefore, his kingdom was split into four parts, just as Daniel prophesied: "Then the goat became exceedingly great, but when he was strong, the great horn was broken, and instead of it there came up four conspicuous horns toward the four winds of heaven" (Dan. 8:8). And again:

> *A mighty king shall arise, who shall rule with great dominion and do as he wills. And as soon as he has arisen, his kingdom shall be broken and divided toward the four winds of heaven, but not to his posterity, nor according to the authority with which he ruled, for his kingdom shall be plucked up and go to others besides these.*
> Daniel 11:3–4

The "goat" and "mighty king" is Alexander the Great. After his death, Alexander's four generals split the kingdom among themselves. Lysimachus took Asia Minor; Cassander, Macedonia; Seleucus, Mesopotamia, Persia, and Levant; and Ptolemy took Egypt and, initially, the region of Palestine—the land encompassing Israel.[82] In the centuries that followed, the Seleucid and Ptolemaic empires fought over control of Israel, since the territory lies at a critical juncture of regions providing strategic and political advantages to the owner. Except for a period starting in the middle of the second century BC and lasting until the Roman conquest in

---

[82] Joshua J. Mark, "The Hellenistic World: The World of Alexander the Great," *Ancient History Encyclopedia*, last modified November 1, 2018, https://www.ancient.eu/article/94/the-hellenistic-world-the-world-of-alexander-theg/.

37 BC, Israel was always subject to some other nation.

Although servitude to foreign entities was familiar ground, the Jewish people longed for the restoration of their kingdom, of a time when they would be free. This was especially true after the taste of independence they had experienced under the Hasmoneans prior to Rome's assertion of control. The prophets Isaiah, Zechariah, and even king David predicted an anointed one, a *Messiah*, who would come and set things right.

The interests of the Judean people were largely political, but who could blame them? They desired autonomy from their neighbors, which would result in freedom from occupation and taxes. Nevertheless, the promise of the Messiah far predates any political predicament God's people could find themselves in. The anointed one was to bring about a moral rescue, freedom from the curse of sin. Millennia before Israel was even a kingdom, we see foreshadows and promises of a Messiah.

Even the third chapter of Genesis contains allusions to the Messiah. To the serpent, God said, "He shall bruise your head, and you shall bruise his heel" (v. 15). The Messiah would come and crush Satan at the cost of his own life. After doling out the consequences of sin to Adam and Eve, God "made for Adam and for his wife garments of skins and clothed them" (v. 21). Where did the skins come from? Most likely from an animal in the garden. God sacrificed an animal to cover the shame of the first couple, symbolizing the sacrifice the Messiah would have to undergo in order to cover our sins.

So a careful study of the Scriptures reveals that God's plan was not to save Israel from occupation. Humanity needed saving much sooner than 586 BC—the year Babylon destroyed the first Temple. From the beginning, God promised one who would destroy the enemy. But no one could have imagined that it would be God himself.

Deus: From Extra to Intra

If you ask me, the incarnation is one of the most amazing realities in all of history. It is unfathomable that God would create a perfect world, that his creation would violate his design leading to death and corruption, and that he would then enter his own creation and subject himself to undeserved pain and suffering on his creation's behalf. It's lunacy.

And yet that's exactly what he did. He found a young woman named Mary to carry Jesus, God's own Son. Jesus was fully human, but he was also fully God in the form of the second person of the Trinity. Do you ever wonder why Jesus came as a baby rather than a full-grown man—or as a man at all? God's ways are his own, but I think there are a couple important factors to consider here. First, God went from outside of the system—we might call this *deus extra machina*—to inside the system, *deus intra machina*. He subjected himself to the sorrows and pain of his own creation brought about by the sins of mankind. Jesus came to undo the curse that we might have life again, and that meant he had to endure the same hardships we do.

As part of this process, Jesus and Mary experienced the first consequence doled out to humanity: "To the woman [God] said, 'I will surely multiply your pain in childbearing; in pain you shall bring forth children'" (Gen. 3:16). From the start, Jesus underwent the ordeal of birth and Mary experienced the pains of pregnancy and labor in order that Immanuel—God with us, God inside the machine—could serve as a proper substitution for us on the cross. Jesus's birth was the first step toward rectifying all that sin had destroyed. And although many in Israel could not believe Jesus was the anointed one, he would, at his death, fulfill the prophecy God uttered in Eden to the serpent in earshot of those fruit-eaters—to crush the head of the enemy and defeat the curse of sin.

You see, God's primary concern is not our present, ephemeral circumstances. He cares about them, yes. But Rome is not his central enemy, nor is it ours. Satan and sin are. Therefore, God wants to bring about salvation from eternal death first and foremost. He wants it so much for us that he entered the machine of his own creation and became like one of us. As Paul reminds us in the book of Philippians:

> *[Jesus], though he was in the form of God, did not count equality with God a thing to be grasped, but emptied himself, by taking the form of a servant, being born in the likeness of men. And being found in human form, he humbled himself by becoming obedient to the point of death, even death on a cross.*
> Philippians 2:6–8

This is the miracle of the incarnation: that Jesus would willingly subject himself to undeserved suffering and punishment that we might have life. Starting with his humble birth in a Judean village, Jesus gave up his godly privilege to become like us, his creation, because of his great love for us.

A Primer on Maintaining Sanity through Suffering

Entering this world through a virgin birth was amazing, but it was just the beginning for Jesus. He had to live a perfect life so that he could serve as a perfect sacrifice for undoing the curse of sin. No pressure. For those of us sinners needing restoration (i.e. everyone), this was our only hope. You might think being a God-man would be an easy task with access to the supernatural at his fingertips. But remember, Jesus willingly limited himself to serve as the role model for humanity. Think you've got it tough or have your fair share of temptations? I'm sure you do. But Jesus had it worse: "We do not have a high priest who is unable to sympathize with our weaknesses, but one who in every respect has been tempted as we are, yet without sin" (Heb. 4:15).

Even before the crucifixion, Jesus's life wasn't exactly a cakewalk. Once he began his ministry and claimed spiritual authority, the Pharisees and other religious leaders tested him *ad nauseam*. More than once they threatened to kill him. Many members of Jesus's own family and hometown rejected him. Though he was an incredible teacher and healer, he had no possessions at the time of his death.

Such a reality should serve as a source of encouragement to us—knowing that whatever type of trial or struggle we could go through, Jesus has already endured it. Have you ever undergone some sort of ordeal and no one around you could relate?

Several years ago I contracted Hand, Foot, and Mouth Disease, a condition caused by a virus. The condition usually affects only young children, but somehow the virus found its way to me. As with many viruses, the effects are magnified in adults. To begin with, I had a fever. Then I experienced the worst sore throat of my life. Every gulp I took felt like I was swallowing razor blades. After a day or two, I developed painful rashes on my feet and ankles. For some reason, my hands remained largely unscathed, but the sores on my feet were so painful I had to sit all day with my feet submerged in an ice bath for as long as I could stand it; it was the only way I could get relief. No medication, topical or oral, seemed to help.

The pain was agonizing, but probably the worst part was that seemingly no one could empathize with my ordeal. Although we had a suspicion I had Hand, Foot, and Mouth, we weren't sure. And since it's pretty rare for adults to catch this virus, those around me couldn't relate to the pain I was experiencing. Yes, Katie was very sympathetic and caring (as always), but still, the experience was isolating. And frustrating.

After a few days with no relief in sight, I finally broke down and drove to the urgent care clinic. But first I had to pull socks up over the sores and then slip my feet into the loosest sneakers I could find. Sitting in the exam room, I pondered whether the trip was a waste of time. I wanted an answer, but I also longed for the ice bath as the pain of unchecked itching forced its way through my central nervous system.

At last, the doc entered and conducted his inspection. With little hesitation and no uncertainty, he said, "You have Hand, Foot, and Mouth Disease." It was a relief to have a diagnosis. Breath bated, I readied myself for the pill or the cream or the shot that would heal me. But any medical professionals reading this already know where this is going.

"Since Hand, Foot, and Mouth is a virus, you'll just have to wait it out. There's nothing I can give you for the condition. Your body will fight it off in seven to ten days," the doctor said. I wasn't sure I would last that long, but my despondency only lasted for a moment. "I had the virus a few years ago, and it was very painful," he continued. "I'm going to write you a prescription to deal with the pain."

Would that doctor have prescribed the opioid if he had never personally battled the virus? I can't say, but I will say the odds are less likely. And being the tough, stubborn man that I am, I don't think I ever even took the narcotic. Quite frankly, seeing a doc who knew exactly how I was feeling was a much stronger relief than any drug. Why? I'm not entirely sure; it doesn't make sense, but maybe it's because the isolating effect of the pain was worse than the pain itself.

Maybe you're struggling with an illness or undergoing a

tremendous hardship. My experience, although awful, was a mere blip on the Richter scale of suffering. But even if you never encounter another human with the same struggles you have, we have a Savior who knows exactly how you feel. He suffered and struggled through the human experience just like we do.

Am I saying that Jesus had Hand, Foot, and Mouth Disease? No, probably not, but Jesus has endured every *type* of suffering and temptation that the human experience can provide. So even though he might have never had that specific virus, he knows what it feels like to be ill and be subject to all the limitations of the human body. He never lost a child, but he knows the loss of death because of his friend Lazarus. Whatever you're dealing with, Jesus knows how it feels—and not just on an intellectual level, but with an intimate, firsthand, experiential knowledge. For specific examples, let's turn to Jesus's temptation in the wilderness.

The Three Most Effective Temptations

Have you ever asked God to strengthen your faith? I have, but I didn't really think through what I was asking for. How else can he strengthen our faith except through testing it? My faith isn't going to get stronger by magic, but instead by opportunities to exercise it. Had I thought things through, maybe I would have been more reserved in asking for a stronger faith.

Jesus, in order to sharpen his resolve, focus, and faith, went into the wilderness at the prompting of the Spirit in order to be tested. But first he had to fast for forty days. I don't know about you, but I get cranky after fasting for four hours. The Scripture, though, tells us he went over a month without food.

As a result, I imagine the first temptation Satan brought upon Jesus must have been pretty enticing. "If you are the Son of God, command these stones to become loaves of bread" (Matt. 4:3). The tempter is shrewd. He loves setting up these false conditions to cause us to stumble. What's the connection between being the Son of God and turning stones to bread? Well, certainly, the Immanuel would have the power to transform rock to rye, no sweat. But is doing so a condition of being God incarnate? Of course not. But Satan was trying to play both to Jesus's physical weakness (hunger) and to the psychological weakness of humanity (pride) in tempting Jesus to prove his divine status.

Jesus didn't take the bait. He responded, "Man shall not live by bread alone, but by every word that comes from the mouth of God" (v. 4). Jesus quoted Deuteronomy here, referencing the manna God provided the Israelites in the wilderness. In doing so, he acknowledged God's role as provider and sustainer of life. Just like God—not Moses—provided water from the rock, as we saw in chapter three, Jesus knew that God would provide the sustenance he needed.

Realizing he couldn't take advantage of Jesus's hunger, Satan tried another play at his pride. He ushered Jesus to the top of the Temple and told him to throw himself down, quoting Psalm 91: "If you are the Son of God, throw yourself down, for it is written, 'He will command his angels concerning you,' and 'On their hands they will bear you up, lest you strike your foot against a stone'" (v. 6).

Do you see what's happening here? It's absolutely true that God would not let the Anointed One perish, but the verse was not an invitation to test God. This is another test Moses failed. We don't know for sure how much Moses knew of his calling at the time, but when he killed the Egyptian, it seems he was trying to force God's hand by starting an insurrection.[83]

---

[83] See Stephen's sermon in Acts 7:23-29 for an interpretation of this event in Exodus 2.

It's no coincidence that Satan took Jesus to the top of the Temple. Throwing himself down and being rescued by angels would have immediately revealed his status as the Messiah. But doing so would not have fit with God's timing or aligned with his will. Jesus would have only been glorifying himself with such an action, not his heavenly Father.

The last temptation smacks of desperation, but is nevertheless enticing. Satan offered Jesus all the kingdoms of the world if he would worship him.[84] This is an appeal to riches and security. It seems ridiculous, but how many of us do stupid things for the promise of wealth and comfort? I know I have. Jesus was vulnerable, starving, and exhausted, and the prospect of untold wealth had to have carried some appeal. It would have to me. And yet, Jesus was secure in his mission and his knowledge of the Scriptures. He responded by quoting Deuteronomy 6:13: "You shall worship the Lord your God and him only shall you serve" (v. 10). And with that, Satan departed and waited for an opportune time to tempt him again.

The trickiness of these temptations is that they all appeal to legitimate needs, and that's how the tempter aims to ensnare you as well. The first, hunger, is obvious. We all need food to survive. Jesus didn't argue against the need for food, but fought back with the reminder that we don't live by food alone, but rather through the sustaining words of God.

The second temptation is esteem. An angel rescue in front of a crowd of religious leaders would have earned Jesus his (correct) title of the Christ, but doing so would have been an illegitimate realization of a legitimate desire. We all need to feel loved, but we must, first and foremost, allow God to fulfill that need.

---

[84] According to Matthew's account. Luke switches Satan's second and third tests. Compare Matthew 4 and Luke 4.

The last temptation is security, one we've already discussed. For Abraham Maslow, security and safety are just above food and water, meaning not much else matters if we don't have some semblance of sanctuary from the elements and other dangers. And yet, we often take fulfilling this legitimate need too far, wrongly assuming money can buy security. Therefore, some people make wealth their number one goal in order to (attempt to) insulate themselves from evil. For Jesus, the promise of the kingdoms of this world meant a life of comfort and security, checking off box number two on Maslow's pyramid. Jesus's response, though? We are to worship God alone. The implication, of course, is that God is the only true and legitimate fulfillment of a real need we have: safety and security. Any attempt to achieve these results outside of his will (e.g. worshiping Satan) is sin.

Our Savior can empathize with our struggles because he lived out the human experience. He endured the limitations of a corrupt world and felt pain and loss like we all do. Satan unloaded his entire clip on Jesus, firing off every temptation he could muster, and Jesus sidestepped every one of them. Unlike you and I, who fall victim to the temptations of this world, Jesus lived a perfect life. But while he passed these three tests at the beginning of his ministry, he continued to deal with the burdens of the day-to-day: stubbed toes, fatigue, stress, perhaps an illness or two. And despite all of these trials, the greatest was yet to come in the form of three spikes and a Roman cross.

The Amazing Story of the Suffering Deity

Jesus made it through Satan's temptations unscathed and innocent as great preparation for ministry on Earth. Nevertheless, the Lord's greatest test was yet to come, and he knew it. In fact, Jesus predicted his own death numerous times to his disciples. Although they couldn't comprehend the implications of Jesus's words, these statements demonstrate that Jesus wasn't taken by surprise at his execution and that he willingly served as a sacrifice on our behalf. His predictions notwithstanding, this latter fact should be obvious, since Jesus made no defense on his behalf despite obvious false testimony against him. In addition, Jesus could have simply avoided Jerusalem, where the heat on him was the hottest, had he desired to avoid crucifixion. And yet again, he could have slipped away from his captors in Gethsemane as he did earlier in Nazareth when the synagogue congregants tried to throw him down a cliff.[85]

Jesus was going to the cross, and he knew it. But that doesn't mean he didn't struggle with his destiny. Just after Satan's third temptation, Scripture tells us that the devil left Jesus and waited for an opportune time to tempt him again.[86] Although the Scripture doesn't explicitly tell us when this occurred, might I offer up a suggestion? Late in his ministry, during one of the instances in which Jesus explained to his disciples that he had to die, Peter protested, saying, "Far be it from you, Lord! This shall never happen to you." Notice Jesus's response: "Get behind me, Satan!" (Matt. 16:22–23). He didn't say, "Get behind me, Peter!" Is it possible this was the opportune time Satan was looking for? And how tempting such a proposition must have been![87] Although Jesus did not hesitate in denouncing Peter's notion, I know I would have been tempted to side with the disciple in hopes of avoiding the agony associated with the cross. This is how Satan operates. He knows when we're at our most vulnerable. He knows when we're most likely to throw in the

---

[85] See Luke 4:16–30.

[86] Luke 4:13.

[87] I am, of course, not the first to suggest this episode as Satan's "opportune time."

towel and surrender to the desires of this world rather than stay true to the Father's will. Jesus didn't take the bait. He recognized the tempter's gambit and quickly dismissed it.

But Gethsemane gives us a peek at Jesus in his most vulnerable state. Though Jesus often slipped away alone to pray, on the night of his arrest, he brought along his disciples for moral support. Yet they could not stay awake to keep watch and pray with the Lord. "Sorrowful, even to death," Jesus fell on his face and asked God to prevent the ordeal he was about to undergo, but only if doing so aligned with the Father's will (Matt. 26:38–39).

God said no.

Within hours, Jesus was dead.

Why the Crown of Thorns Backfired on the Romans

Jesus wasn't the first person the Romans crucified. The Empire most likely adopted crucifixion after learning of the practice from the Phoenicians during the Punic Wars starting in 246 BC.[88] Jesus wasn't the last person to be crucified, either. The practice persisted until emperor Constantine outlawed it in the fourth century. Yet, by the time of Christ, the Romans had perfected the art of brutality and spared none of it when it came to our Lord.

The Sanhedrin spit on Jesus, slapped him, and struck him. Then, Roman soldiers stripped him naked and scourged him with a barbed whip designed to rip flesh from its victims with every blow. If that wasn't enough, the soldiers then humiliated Jesus by dressing him in a scarlet robe and handing him a staff in mockery of his claim to be

---

[88] F. P. Retief and L. Cilliers, "History of Medicine: The History and Pathology of Crucifixion," *South African Medical Journal,* 93, no. 12 (2008): 141, accessed February 8, 2021, http://www.samj.org.za/index.php/samj/article/view/2462/1710.

king. Then they ripped the staff from his hand, beat him with it, and spit on him. And all of this before the crucifixion even began.

But let's not forget the crown of thorns. In conjunction with robe and staff, the Romans twisted thorns together to fashion a crown and jammed it onto Jesus's brow. With the blood spilling down Christ's face, I doubt if any of the onlookers realized the irony of their act. Of course, the crown of thorns was ironic; it was meant to be. Jesus said he was king, but the Romans and Jews didn't believe it. So rather than a real crown, they made one out of sharp plant material as a way to mock him.

But there's another layer of irony that, no doubt, escaped everyone present that day. When God entered the machine of his own creation in form of Immanuel, Jesus of Nazareth, he and Mary endured the first consequence of the fall of mankind. Pain in childbirth was woman's punishment for disobedience in the garden of Eden. So as mother and child suffered through the contractions of labor, Jesus took the first step in assuming the role as atoner and perfect representative of humanity.

But what was man's punishment? Take a look:

> *To Adam he said, "Because you listened to your wife and ate fruit from the tree about which I commanded you, 'You must not eat from it,'*
>
> > *"Cursed is the ground because of you;*
> > *through painful toil you will eat food from it*
> > *all the days of your life.*
> > *It will produce thorns and thistles for you,*
> > *and you will eat the plants of the field."*
>
> Genesis 3:17–18

Did you catch that? Adam's punishment was thorns. So when the Roman soldiers twisted the thorns into a crown and forced it upon

Jesus's brow—implanting it deep into his flesh—at that moment, Jesus bore man's punishment in a literal sense.

Because of our disobedience, we were separated from God, given thorns and birthing pains instead. Yet Jesus came that we might be reconciled to the Father. He took our punishment even though he was innocent and willingly gave his life as a sacrifice so that we could live.

The Romans intended the crown of thorns for mockery. God intended it for redemption.

But the worst was yet to come. Already bloodied and brutalized, Jesus was nailed to a beam by his wrists and feet. Then the Romans lifted up the cross and implanted it into a prepared hole in the ground. Now gravity was the enemy. With all of their body weight supported by three nails, victims of crucifixion had to push themselves up by their feet in order to get a breath. As the hours wore on, eventually—sometimes days later—the crucified became too exhausted to strive for air. As a result, asphyxiation was the typical cause of death.

The Hardest Thing about Christ's Crucifixion

I'd rather have been crucified. That's the thought I had in my head one morning in the shower. A few months ago, my pastor preached a moving sermon using the Forty Martyrs of Sebaste as an illustration—a story I had not heard before.

Let me briefly tell it here:

A group of Christian soldiers in the fourth century AD were condemned to death because of their professed faith in Christ. Rather than a simple execution, these men were to be stripped and escorted to the middle of a frozen pond (although they willingly disrobed and ran to the pond of their own accord). At the shore was a warm bath for anyone ready to denounce Jesus.

In all, forty men froze to death as martyrs for Christ.

I was reminded of the story that morning because I wasn't in the shower but a few minutes when the hot water began to fail. I thought about how unbearable a cold shower would be on a winter morning—even with a furnace heating our home. I thought about how impossible it would be to stand there in the cold. I wondered if I would betray Jesus for a warm bath.

That's when I had the thought.

I'd rather have been crucified than forced to stand naked on a frozen pond with a warm bath taunting my pain. But immediately I felt ashamed. I had disrespected Jesus and devalued the cross. I had minimized the pain that he had to endure on my behalf when I knew I couldn't even stand a five-minute cold shower. Then I asked myself, *Why? Why would I rather be crucified?*

The answer is quite simple, and it led me to a greater understanding of Christ's death. Were I nailed to a cross, I would not have the option to get down. My flesh could not betray me once I was pinned down to the pine. The Forty Martyrs of Sebaste, on the other hand, could have at any point denounced God and immediately had comfort from their suffering. That's when it hit me.

Jesus could have done the same. At any point during his suffering, he could have ended it. He could have thought, *You know what? You all aren't worth it. Why should I have to endure this?* He could have come down from that cross at any point. He could have saved himself. As he said, "Do you think I cannot call on my Father, and he will at once put at my disposal more than twelve legions of angels?" (Matt. 26:53).

He could have saved himself.

But he didn't.

You see, the suffering he endured was bad enough, but he wasn't just fighting the pain. He was fighting his own flesh, because everything in him had to be screaming, *Put a stop to this.* It would be a bit like placing your hand on a hot stove and then leaving it there despite every impulse and reflex in your body begging you—commanding you—to pull it back. But he didn't do it because he knew his death had a purpose. He knew his death meant that we might be saved if we would only put our faith in him.[89] So don't forget this fact about Christ's death. It demonstrates just how much love God really has for us.

One Thing Worse than Crucifixion

You might think crucifixion is the worst possible thing that could happen to someone. And you might be right if your context is the physical world. Jesus's death was as violent and painful as they come. Execution on a cross was so brutal, it gave us the word *excruciating* to describe pain like that "from the cross." But Jesus actually underwent something much worse than crucifixion: he was rejected by God.

Compared to rejection, the physical pain was but a paper cut. As a substitute for our sins, Jesus experienced both a physical death and a sort of spiritual death—separation from God. This is why Jesus quoted Psalm 22 while on the cross: "My God, my God, why have you forsaken me?" (v. 1). Yes, physical pain is bad, but separation from God is even worse. It is unbearable and unsustainable, because God is life itself. Separation from life, by definition, leads to death.

As weird and amazing as the story of a suffering deity is, God's decision wasn't random. It wasn't spontaneous or reactionary. Jesus deliberately endured the cross for at least two reasons. The first is so

---

[89] See John 3:16, for example.

he could experience the human condition. Jesus came to be the perfect representation of man. Where Adam failed, Jesus succeeded, and he is our role model for life. *What Would Jesus Do?*, although cliché today, is a legitimate question that, when pondered in honesty and sincerity, will not lead you astray. In this experience, Jesus can empathize firsthand with every type of suffering you and I could ever endure. I don't know about you, but that brings me some level of comfort.

Second, Jesus allowed himself to be mocked and marred beyond recognition so he could assume the punishment we should have received. In Paul's famous axiom in Romans, he wrote, "For the wages of sin is death" (6:23). As a result of our acts of disobedience, we earn death. But God, because of his tremendous love for us, sent his Son to die in our place, to take the punishment we rightly deserved. While the Romans thought they were killing an insurrectionist, they were really enabling the greatest kingdom ever established. While the Judeans thought they were ridding the world of a false messiah, Jesus's death enabled salvation for the entire world. And while Satan may have thought he had defeated his greatest enemy, the coming resurrection would signal the beginning of the end for the tempter—a crushing defeat in fulfillment of Genesis 3:15: "He will crush your head, and you will strike his heel" (NIV). If God entering his own creation was an unbelievable act, the pain of the cross superseded that incredulity. Nevertheless, as you know, the story doesn't end at Calvary.

Your Only Reason for Hope in a World Full of Suffering

A few years ago, I thought my mom was dead. Along with other family members, I watched as her heart stopped for nearly a minute on the cardiac floor of Norman Regional Hospital. Had she not been there to receive external defibrillation that night, she would have died. As the chirping heart monitor filled the room with its dreadful alarms, I remember feeling the blood drain from my head and a knot seize up in my gut. Sweat broke out on my brow. I had to sit down to avoid passing out myself.

What happens when you die? Ask a naturalist and you'll get a simple answer: nothing. Life cannot persist outside of the mortal body because the only thing that matters is matter. You're just a conglomeration of atoms and molecules. Nothing more. The Christian, of course, has a much different answer.

Regardless, nearly everyone has a similar reaction to death—especially the death of a loved one. We feel sadness, pain, and surprise, and sometimes we just plain pass out. A skeptic might use this as evidence against the afterlife; why do we all have similar reactions to death if there is life after death?

When God created man on the sixth day, he gave him dominion over the earth. God charged Adam with naming the animals and tasked him with tending to the garden. Mankind was to rule over the plants and animals.[90] Man was supposed to bring order. And, of course, death was not part of God's design. Sin made death a reality. And death is one thing we cannot control, no matter how hard we try.

"You will not certainly die," Satan said to Eve as she lusted after the forbidden fruit. Yes, you certainly will die. And there's nothing you can do about it. Death is a reminder of sin, of the fallen nature of our flesh. That's part of why Christians react with sorrow at the death of a loved one.

But for an atheist, that sorrow is deeper. It is permanent. Death marks the end of the road. Paul wrote about this distinction in his

---

[90] Genesis 1:28–29.

first letter to the Corinthians. He wrote, "If Christ has not been raised, your faith is futile; you are still in your sins. Then those also who have fallen asleep in Christ are lost. If only for this life we have hope in Christ, we are of all people most to be pitied" (15:17–19 NIV).

Of course, he's right. If Christ was not raised, then we Christians are, perhaps, the most pathetic creatures on the planet. Why? Because we are deluding ourselves into thinking that suffering has meaning, that pain has a resolution, and that what has been lost can be restored. But we know that Jesus *did* rise, and by conquering the grave he fulfilled the promise of hope he offers to those who put their faith in him.

How to Prove That Man Is More than Molecules

Here's one reason why Jesus had to rise from the dead: rising from the dead in bodily form was the ultimate proof that Jesus was who he said he was.

With science, we can do some incredible things: cloning, nuclear reaction, space travel. But try bringing a person back to life who's been dead for three days. Better yet: try dying and then bringing yourself back after three days.

Jesus's resurrection was the ultimate proof that God does, indeed, exist and that Jesus was who he said he was. Because if Jesus did, in fact, die—and all reliable historical accounts (even extrabiblical accounts) note that he *did* die—then there is no other possible explanation for the resurrection except that there exists something outside of the physical, observable universe.

That something is God.

He's real. He raised his Son from the grave. And he did it so that everyone—atheists and theists alike—might believe in him and live.

In light of the knowledge of the resurrection, we understand that suffering is temporary for those who believe in him. In fact, Jesus is our only hope in a world full of pain and injustice. As our resurrected Savior, he will return in the last days to set everything right, and once his will is accomplished, all believers will be restored to new life in heaven with God for eternity.

In the throes of hardship, it's difficult to visualize this reality because the concept is foreign to us. But we must view suffering through the prism of eternity. When we do, we recognize the relative nature of our duration on earth. Albert Einstein once explained relativity this way: "When you sit with a nice girl for two hours you think it's only a minute, but when you sit on a hot stove for a minute you think it's two hours. That's relativity."[91]

Life can often feel like a hot stove, whether in the day-to-day trials of paper cuts, exhaustion, and financial stress or in the tragic events like miscarriages, automobile accidents, or abuse. But because of the resurrection, we have hope for eternity, which will make the hardships of this life seem like a mere blip on the radar of existence. Because when forever is your reality, seventy-five years is infinitesimal. As James wrote, "You are a mist that appears for a little time and then vanishes" (4:14). So while this red-hot stove of a life might seem to last forever, remember that we will have rest from our suffering. How do I know? Because despite the brutality of the cross, Christ's tomb is empty.

---

[91] "Einstein Is Found Hiding on Birthday: Busy With Gift Microscope," *New York Times* (New York), Mar. 15, 1929.

CHAPTER 10
The Most Effective Christians Live Their Lives This Way

Grace never seems fair until you need some.
—Bob Goff[92]

The best way to live life to the fullest.

If you've been alive for any amount of time, you know this life is difficult. I don't care if you were born into wealth with a trust fund in your name and a golden crib in your nursery. As we've seen, illness, accidents, natural disasters, and the general fallen nature of humanity leaves no one exempt from suffering at some point in their lives.

Unfortunately, many turn to Christ with the expectation that these problems will all disappear once they accept Jesus and receive salvation. Don't get me wrong: Jesus offers new life and eternal security for those who turn to him. As the prophet Joel wrote, "Everyone who calls on the name of the LORD shall be saved" (2:32). Nevertheless, to expect that, once we're saved, all of our problems will evaporate is unrealistic and sets one up for disillusionment.

---

[92] Bob Goff, *Everybody, Always: Becoming Love in a World Full of Setbacks and Difficult People* (Nashville: Nelson Books, 2018), Kindle edition, 205.

If anything, Jesus seems to suggest that suffering will *increase* once we're attached to Christ's name. Just as Jesus received testing, temptation, and abuse, we too are not immune. As Jesus said, "If they persecuted me, they will also persecute you" (Jn. 15:20). Some might ask: what's the benefit of surrendering your life to Jesus? Oh, you mean aside from eternal bliss with our creator in heaven? How much space do I have? In our context, Jesus offers peace in tumult, joy in sorrow, and grace through tribulation. And, as we discussed already, Christians can derive meaning from adversity in various ways. Trials can serve many purposes. One is to serve as a reminder of the promise of glory in heaven. Another is to provide opportunities to strengthen our faith and our reliance on God. Yet another is to serve as a witness of God's goodness to unbelievers. Since we all endure hardship, those who rely on God's grace to make it through will be light on Jesus's hilltop city, shining bright for others to see.

Effective Christians don't live in dread or pessimism at the prospect of suffering, but they acknowledge that they aren't immune to it, either. Nevertheless, there is one trap which threatens to ensnare even the best of us.

How to Combat Bitterness

If there's one thing holding many Christians back from living for God's glory, it's bitterness. Bitterness is harboring persistent ill will toward someone in response to a wrong. Regardless of the type of hardship—whether an intentional slight or happenstance such as a natural disaster—it is easy to fall into this trap. When a fellow human wrongs us, the object of our scorn is an easy target. And probably deserved. But sometimes tragedy tempts us to blame God. I had a coworker once tell me that her husband was mad at God for some premature deaths in his family.

Bitterness is rampant in all religions and cultures, not just Christianity. Problem is, we're explicitly commanded to avoid it. Paul wrote, "Let all bitterness and wrath and anger and clamor and slander be put away from you, along with all malice" (Eph. 4:31). The essence of bitterness is the inability or unwillingness to forgive a wrong. Yet it is impossible to live your purpose and harbor bitterness in your heart. As John wrote: "Whoever claims to love God yet hates a brother or sister is a liar. For whoever does not love their brother and sister, whom they have seen, cannot love God, whom they have not seen" (1 Jn. 4:20 NIV). You can't glorify God without loving him, and you can't love him without loving others. Can bitterness and love coexist?

Although I'd rather not share, I'd be a hypocrite if I didn't disclose that I'm working through some resentment in my professional career at the very moment I type this. Actually, I'd love to share all the seedy details with you. I'd love to get you on my side in the invisible battle against my employer. Misery loves company, and I'd love for you to share in my outrage. This is the essence of bitterness; continuous feelings of hatred in response to injury or insult. I even have daydreams about one day getting revenge once I have the necessary leverage. It feels so good and so bad all at the same time.

The antidote to bitterness is forgiveness. Yet forgiving does not mean endorsing bad behavior. Instead, forgiveness frees you from anger and the offender from his debt. It's not a matter of guilt or innocence. Of course the offender is guilty, but you free them anyway in light of the forgiveness you have received. But what if he or she is unrepentant? This makes things much more difficult, for sure, but take comfort in the knowledge that while God is merciful, he is also just. God will right all wrongs. It's not our place to punish the unjust.

When we harbor bitterness, we do so as a punitive measure, but even if bitterness were godly, it's rarely effective. Often, the person we try to punish has no awareness of our hatred or simply doesn't care. And even if you succeed in inducing a feeling of guilt in the criminal, in all cases bitterness causes far more damage to the bearer than to its target. So how do you deal with it? The first step is to acknowledge the truth from the book of Romans that "all have sinned and fall short of the glory of God" (3:23). We've all messed up. We've all hurt people in our lives.

The second step is to remember Calvary. Not only have we all sinned, but Christ took the punishment and the blame for our sins. That's how much he loves us. And even while suffering agony on the cross, he prayed one of the most powerful prayers ever uttered: "Father, forgive them, for they do not know what they are doing" (Lk. 23:34 NIV). Here we see our Lord showing grace to the very people who mocked him, spit on him, tore the flesh off his back, and drove nails through his hands and feet, leaving him to suffocate. Kind of puts things into perspective, huh? Let Christ be your model and cast aside your bitterness.

Spend time on your knees in prayer. Ask your friends and your pastor to pray for you. As hard as it is, forgiveness gladdens God's heart. As Jesus said in the Sermon on the Mount, "Blessed are the merciful, for they will be shown mercy" (Matt. 5:7 NIV).

With bitterness as your companion, you can't glorify God. Instead, you'll waste away. Don't spoil the precious few moments you have on earth in anger. Instead, remember what Jesus did for you and trust that he will make things right.

If it seems unnatural and bizarre to let go of bitterness, well, it is. Remember, bitterness is a reaction against some type of wrong, whether real or perceived. So when something happens that shouldn't happen to us, we want restoration. We want justice—for the wrong to be righted. But forgiveness means releasing the offender from the debt. This is unnatural. It feels so wrong. But isn't this exactly how God operates?

Again, let's go back to Jesus for a moment. While on the cross, he prayed that God would forgive his torturers while he was being tortured. Incredible. That doesn't seem right, does it? In the same way, God offers grace—unmerited favor—to anyone who repents and asks for forgiveness. Such an offer, quite frankly, is unnatural too. It doesn't make sense. I like the way author and speaker Bob Goff puts it. He wrote that "grace never seems fair until you need some." In reality, grace is never fair, even when we need some. But that's the good news of the gospel, isn't it?

My pastor once said that God's grace should disturb you. That a man could rape and murder a young girl and then later come to God on his knees and receive forgiveness is wrong. It's unfair. It's disturbing. Now, in this life, said man would (and should) go to prison for life, but in the beyond? Just like the thief crucified with Jesus who admitted he deserved his punishment, the repentant rapist will enter paradise with you and me. God's grace is simultaneously the most wonderful and most disturbing reality. It means those who don't deserve forgiveness receive it. But it also means those who don't deserve forgiveness receive it.

Yet forgiveness isn't Jesus's only unnatural teaching. We have spoken quite a bit about blessings throughout this book. When most people hear the word *blessed*, they think of it in worldly terms: wealth, health, peace from enemies, or a large, happy family. There's nothing wrong with these things, and I agree that they are blessings, but Jesus gave us a radical alternative to what it means to be blessed.

In the Sermon on the Mount, Jesus offered up nine different blessings that, for the most part, sound awful, if I'm being honest. Here's what he said:

> *Blessed are the poor in spirit, for theirs is the kingdom of heaven.*
> *Blessed are those who mourn, for they shall be comforted.*

Blessed are the meek, for they shall inherit the earth.
Blessed are those who hunger and thirst for righteousness, for
they shall be satisfied.
Blessed are the merciful, for they shall receive mercy.
Blessed are the pure in heart, for they shall see God.
Blessed are the peacemakers, for they shall be called sons of God.
Blessed are those who are persecuted for righteousness' sake, for
theirs is the kingdom of heaven.
Blessed are you when others revile you and persecute you and
utter all kinds of evil against you falsely on my account. Rejoice
and be glad, for your reward is great in heaven, for so they
persecuted the prophets who were before you.
Matthew 5:3–12

Jesus said we are blessed if we are poor in spirit, if we mourn, if we are meek, if we hunger for righteousness, if we are merciful, if we are pure in heart, if we are peacemakers, if we are persecuted, and if we are slandered. I'm cool with striving to be pure in heart and thirsting for righteousness, but I really don't want to have to mourn, be persecuted, or be slandered.

Of course, we need to make a distinction here. For some of these Beatitudes, Jesus wasn't teaching that we should seek out such circumstances. He wasn't instructing his followers to find opportunities for others to "utter all kinds of evil against you falsely" (Matt 5:11). Instead, Jesus knew that those who follow him and serve God would be slandered. He taught that when these things happen, we should not despair, but should instead be happy because God will reward those who suffer on his account. So while blessing as defined by this world and the Old Testament way of thinking focuses only on the here and now—wealth, power, health, esteem, sex, drugs, and rock and roll—Jesus provided his followers with a long view of blessing. He taught that the reward in heaven would be great for those who undergo these trials. So for many of these states, we should not seek them out, but instead not be surprised or disappointed when they come. Embrace them, knowing that, while earthly riches and other such blessings will pass away, heavenly rewards will endure for eternity. Taking this long view makes suffering all the more palatable.

Undoubtedly, Peter and the other apostles whom the high priest arrested recalled Christ's teachings. Not long after the resurrection, the religious leaders arrested some apostles for proclaiming Christ to the people. But that night, an angel opened the doors of the prison and instructed them to continue teaching in the Temple courts the next day. Upon discovering that the apostles had been freed from prison, the chief priests once again brought them before the council. This time, after some discussion, they beat the apostles and let them go. How did the beaten men respond? With exuberance. Luke reports, "They left the presence of the council, rejoicing that they were counted worthy to suffer dishonor for the name" (Acts 5:41). This reaction would seem like the behavior of mad men had we not both the words and actions of Jesus himself to which we can hearken back. They knew that their reward was the kingdom of heaven—something of much more value than physical well-being.

This type of mindset is difficult. Even for those of us who are convinced of the veracity of the Beatitudes—that the persecuted are actually blessed—we are still bound in many respects to this corrupted body in a fallen world. Pain hurts. (You can quote me on that.) Remember Maslow's hierarchy of needs? Maslow said that the basic needs of food, safety, and security must be met before we can attend to other needs.[93] This isn't rocket science. Caught in a hailstorm, a man will probably seek shelter before working on

---

[93] McLeod, "Maslow's Hierarchy of Needs."

improving his marriage. He's got two needs: a need for an intimate relationship with his wife and a need to not get bloodied by baseball-sized chunks of ice falling at fifty-five miles per hour. Which one do you think takes precedence?

The directive to embrace persecution and pick up a cross to follow Jesus is a bit like holding a marriage counseling session in a hailstorm. Jesus subverts the Maslow pyramid, skipping over basic needs in favor of heavenly aims. It would have been safer for the apostles (physically) to skip town and go back to Bethany or Galilee, or just about anywhere other than Jerusalem, after their release from prison than to obey the word of God and return to the Temple to preach. Instead, they obeyed, disregarding their safety in favor of eternal rewards.

(Note: I am not claiming that you should let yourself get hurt for no reason at all. I *am* saying that there will be times when you must sacrifice some comfort, some esteem, or some level of security for the sake of the gospel.)

The problem, of course, is our flesh and blood. Biologically, every instinct within us tells to avoid pain and to fill our bellies as early and often as possible. Our primitive fears guide us to make every provision to ensure safety at every turn. We refuse to take any other action until those Maslowian needs are satisfied. The Beatitudes, on the other hand, remind us that there are things much better, higher, and more fulfilling than bodily comfort and security. Compared to the glory of eternity, what's a little persecution? Wouldn't you rather be filled with righteousness than with calories?

In laying out these Beatitudes, Jesus radically redefined success for his followers. The blessed are not those who have mountains of cash or modern comforts or conflict-free, tragedy-free lives. Instead, Jesus defined success with his sights set squarely on the eternal. Society may look down upon the pure in heart, but these people will see God.[94] Those who focus on comfort might experience it for a season, but lasting comfort comes to those who mourn.[95] There's no do doubt that success for the Christian looks different than it does for the non-Christian. How else could you explain the praise on the lips of the apostles who received a beating for the sake of Jesus? Were they just delusional? No; they saw the resurrected Christ and knew that, because of Jesus, their suffering was temporary and their future blessings eternal.

But let's go back to mourning for a moment. Why did Jesus specifically mention those who mourn? Some commentators, such as nineteenth-century theologian Edward Plumptre, argue that Jesus was talking about those who mourn their sin. He wrote, "The 'mourning' is not the sorrow of the world . . . but the sorrow which flows out in the tears that cleanse, the mourning over sin itself and the stain which it has left upon the soul."[96] In other words, God will comfort those who feel remorse for their sins.

I agree with this sentiment, but I believe the Beatitude goes deeper. Mourning is both an acknowledgement and a reminder that things aren't as they should be. Mourning only happens in a world with sin. Death was not part of God's original design, but sin ushered in bodily death. So to mourn a loved one specifically is to mourn the effects of sin more generally. Those who mourn understand this on an intimate level, and Jesus looks ahead to the time of permanent

---

[94] Matthew 5:8.

[95] Matthew 5:4.

[96] E. H. Plumptre, *The Gospel According to St. Matthew*, Ellicott's Commentary for English Readers, ed. Charles Ellicott (London: Cassel and Co., 1880), 48, digitized version, https://babel.hathitrust.org/cgi/pt?id=uva.x000418966&view=1up&seq=1 .

restoration of joy, life, and peace in heaven for those who call on his name.

Our friend Solomon commented on mourning too. In Ecclesiastes 7:2, he wrote, "It is better to go to the house of mourning than to go to the house of feasting, for this is the end of all mankind, and the living will lay it to heart." I like how the New Living Translation puts it: "Better to spend your time at funerals than at parties. After all, everyone dies—so the living should take this to heart." Can you imagine the morbid soul who scans the obituaries for funeral services as a way to spend his free time? What's Solomon getting at? Is he out of his mind?

It is unclear whether or not Solomon believed in the afterlife. He seems unsure when he wrote, "Who knows whether the spirit of man goes upward and the spirit of the beast goes down into the earth?" (Eccl. 3:21). Yet toward the end of Ecclesiastes he seems to affirm the afterlife when he wrote, "The spirit returns to God who gave it" (12:7).

Regardless of his views on what happens after death, Solomon's advice here is sound. Whatever it takes for men and women to contemplate their mortality is a bonus. Partying, as fun as it is, focuses only on the here and now. It is about feeling good in the moment with food, drink, and fellowship. Yet when a person thinks on her mortality, it requires her to ponder what kind of life she wants to lead—the lasting legacy of her life.

Will Anyone Regret Your Death?

Have you read Stephen Covey's *The 7 Habits of Highly Successful People*? The first chapter alone will change your life.

The author asks you to imagine your own funeral. You write your own eulogy. You imagine what your spouse, coworkers, friends, siblings, and anyone else who matters to you would say at your death. This powerful exercise forces you to take a hard look at what you really value, at what's important to you in life. The hope is that, in doing so, you won't end up like Jehoram.

There were a lot of nasty kings in the Old Testament, and Jehoram was one of them. There's only a short chapter on his life: he did evil in the eyes of the Lord and he slaughtered all his brothers so they wouldn't challenge his throne. You know, typical king stuff. Because of his wickedness, he ended up with only one son, a painful disease of the bowels (his bowels literally "came out"), and a nation in shambles.

Then he died.

He's a forgettable man, yes, but there's a powerful statement at the end of Jehoram's story that made me pause: "His people made no funeral fire in his honor, as they had for his predecessors. . . . He passed away, to no one's regret" (2 Chron. 21:19b, 20b NIV). Jehoram died in great pain, alone, and no one even cared.

So here's my question—my challenge—to you (and to myself): will anyone regret your death? Will you live your life for yourself, or will you spend it in service to others? Will you do work that matters, parent your children like never before, and invest in other people? Or will you invest in more television?

Imagine your funeral years from now. What do you want to have accomplished? What kind of relationships do you want to have had? How you answer these questions demonstrates what's truly valuable to you. Write them down so you don't forget them. It's so easy to get distracted by the bright lights of the world. Television, cars, power, pride, and prestige are all distractions the enemy is trying to use to derail you from making your life matter.

So this is my plea to you: identify what's important to you and invest in those things. Work tirelessly to make sure that if you died tomorrow, there would be a few folks who'd be sad you're no longer around. And if you need inspiration, I'm sure I could help you find a few funerals in your area to attend.

Whatever you imagine your funeral to be like or however you would like your life to play out, there is one principle, I believe, all effective Christians work toward. The principle manifests itself in many ways. We can describe it as moving from an inward focus to an outward focus. We can call it living as one who is proactive rather than reactive. But perhaps this is the best way to describe it: effective Christians move from focusing on sins of commission to sins of omission.

You see, many people outside of Christianity see our religion as burdensome and legalistic. They envision that turning to Christ comes with a set of rules and limitations on what they can do. No dancing. No movies. No alcohol. No fun. You get the point. Now, don't get me wrong, there are many churches around the world whose lists of rules are stifling, but this is not what true Christianity is about.

Yes, there are hard-and-fast rules, especially regarding sexuality, which many refuse to abide by and therefore turn away from God. But for those who turn to Christ, we accept the moral framework laid forth by the Bible. Yet even the most disciplined person still struggles with sin in some ways. I'm talking about lying, gossiping, cheating on your taxes, lusting, eating too much, and so on. Notice what all of these things have in common; they are all acts we commit which go against the will of God. They are all negative commands: "you shall not give false testimony" and "you shall not commit adultery," for a couple of examples (see Exodus 20:14, 16). Negative commands tell us what not to do, and these are the rules that many outsiders think Christianity is all about.

It's not hard to see why people come to this conclusion. For many

Christians, this is all they ever focus on—the shall nots. These are called sins of commission: doing something that violates God's commands. They get caught in a cycle of sin, whether it be pornography, rage, gluttony, gossip, or whatever. All of their efforts are used up trying not to commit sin. It's an admirable fight, but it's not the approach effective Christians take.

The Only Way to Remove Darkness from Your Life

The older I get, the more I recognize the universality of the axiom, "nature abhors a vacuum." Want to know where to find my children? Go to whichever room is the tidiest. Once they've wrecked it, they move on to the next. They never play in their bedrooms unless the areas are clean. Once the space is sufficiently cluttered, they'll search for a neater space.

But this isn't just true of children and play areas.

The newly retired quickly find their calendars fuller than when they had a job.

In weather systems, high pressure always flows to low pressure.

Adding more lanes to the freeway should alleviate traffic, right? Well, maybe not. Research shows that increasing throughput might actually promote congestion.[97]

It seems that in many areas of life, vacuums—which we'll loosely define as empty spaces or the lack of something—are unnatural and unstable. They don't last. We give the Greek philosopher Aristotle credit for first coming up with this principle, even though he never said the words "nature abhors a vacuum." This phrasing seems to have originated with the French writer François Rabelais in the sixteenth century.

---

[97] Adam Mann, "What's Up with That: Building Bigger Roads Actually Makes Traffic Worse," Wired, Condé Nast, June 17, 2014, https://www.wired.com/2014/06/wuwt-traffic-induced-demand/.

Where am I going with this? This book is by no means a science book, but I think the principle applies to our spiritual lives too. In fact, Jesus told a parable to a similar effect:

> *When the unclean spirit has gone out of a person, it passes through waterless places seeking rest, but finds none. Then it says, "I will return to my house from which I came." And when it comes, it finds the house empty, swept, and put in order. Then it goes and brings with it seven other spirits more evil than itself, and they enter and dwell there, and the last state of that person is worse than the first. So also will it be with this evil generation.*
> Matthew 12:43–45

Do you see what happened here? When the evil spirit left, the person did not fill the once-occupied space, and he therefore created a void in his life. As a result, it was only a matter of time before that vacuum would be filled. It's easy to overlook this parable, but we shouldn't miss out on the message here. How many people are only looking to remove the evil from their lives? Once the illness or bad work situation or sin is removed, we're left with a vacuum. Try as we might, we can't operate with such a void in our lives, so it's only a matter of time before drama moves back in and brings its buddies.

Instead of simply asking God to remove the bad things from our lives, may we seek to fill ourselves with the Spirit. Then, when sin tries to move back into our lives, it will find there's no room. Think of it this way: light isn't the absence of darkness; darkness is the absence of light. In the same way, Christianity isn't about removing evil from your life as much as it is filling your life with righteousness. As a wise person once said, "Jesus did not come into the world to make bad men good. He came into the world to make dead men live."[98] And as Jesus himself said, "I came that they may have life and have it abundantly" (Jn. 10:10).

How do we live an abundant life? There's another type of sin that is rarely talked about or paid attention to. It is called sin of omission. A sin of omission is when you fail to do something that God wanted you to do. A classic example is Jonah, to whom God said, "Go to Nineveh." Jonah responded, "Nope!" Now, for us, the commands are *usually* not so specific, but they are still there. Unlike sins of commission, these errors result from not following positive commands. Here are some easy examples: "Remember the Sabbath day" and "Honor your father and your mother" (Ex. 20:8, 12). Therefore, to the Israelites, doing something like working on the Sabbath was sin of omission; the act of work itself was not a sin, but doing so on the Sabbath caused the worker to fail to honor the holy day. See how this works?

Now, of course, we can't ever free ourselves fully from sins of commission. There's always the temptation to gossip about someone you don't like, tell a white lie to avoid unpleasant consequences, or gaze a little too long at that man or woman on the screen. Even Paul struggled. He wrote, "I do not do what I want, but I do the very thing I hate" (Rom. 7:15).

So don't think you're ever free of the temptation to perform sins of commission. It's at the moment you believe you are least vulnerable that you're probably the most vulnerable. Always keep your guard up against temptation. As 1 Peter 5:8 advises, "Be sober-minded; be watchful. Your adversary the devil prowls around like a roaring lion, seeking someone to devour." And please don't think I'm advocating giving up the fight against sins of commission. I'm not.

---

[98] Although many attribute this quotation to evangelist and author Leonard Ravenhill, I have been unable to track down an authoritative source for this quotation.

Many of us must wrestle with our own issues before we can turn our focus outward. I get that.

Nevertheless, I'm convinced that the most effective Christians on earth are proactive in their approach. Rather than trying *not* to do something, they set out to accomplish the will of God. These need not be grand acts of faith, but they can be. Usually, these are simple things, like studying God's Word, spending time in prayer, or volunteering to wipe noses in the three-year-old Sunday School room when nobody else wants to so their parents can hear from God in the Sunday service.

Jesus gave both negative and positive commands to his followers. But when he was questioned on the greatest commandment, he endorsed two, both positive: "Love the Lord your God with all your heart and with all your soul and with all your mind" and "Love your neighbor as yourself" (Matt. 22:37, 39). Failing to do these things, as hard as they may be, constitute sins of omission. Would you rather sleep in for a few more minutes or spend a few minutes each morning with God? Would you rather pretend your neighbor doesn't need help unloading bags of mulch or offer to help? Would you rather serve on Sunday or let someone else do it?

Christians who want to make a difference try their hardest to seek out God's will for their lives and then act on it. They give generously of their money and time. They do the right thing even when no one's watching. They seek out opportunities to advance the kingdom. These are the people who make this terrible world a better place. These are the people whose deaths we will regret.

People commit sins of omission for a variety of reasons, such as fear and laziness, among others. These excuses are tools in Satan's belt to prevent us from living our most effective lives for Christ. The tempter knows that spending time with God is the best way to discern his will for your life.

Your Utmost Isn't Enough, but It's All God Wants

No matter how hard you try, no matter how disciplined you are, your utmost isn't enough. As imperfect people living in a sinful, fallen world, we will mess up. Those around us will hurt us, even if it's unintentional. Natural disasters and terminal illnesses will befall us and those we love.

Yes, it's true, your utmost isn't enough to earn heaven or prevent tragedy, but it's all God wants from you. He wants you to love him with everything you've got. He wants you to treat those around you with the same love, dignity, and respect that you would like. Your utmost may not be enough, but that's okay . . . because God's grace is.

God's grace is enough to cover every sin, every mistake. God's grace can help you through dark times and restore you to a status even better than before, just like he did for Job. How? It's as Jesus told Martha on that grim day when he visited Lazarus's corpse: "I am the resurrection and the life" (Jn. 11:25). Jesus became a human, lived a sinless life, and died a torturous and sacrificial death on our behalf so he might cover for us where our utmost fails. On the third day, he rose from the tomb and later ascended into heaven, thereby conquering death and undoing the curse brought upon us by the fall in Eden. He did all this because he loves us.

In response, we must give our utmost for his highest. But don't do so with the illusion that it will be enough. Instead, anticipate the mistakes and the heartache knowing that where we fall, God's grace is enough.

Don't forget your free gift!
12 Things Effective Christians Do (Even When Life Isn't Going as Planned)

Don't forget to download your free guide to the secrets of effective Christian living.

You'll get a sweet PDF detailing twelve practices and habits common among world-changing Christ-followers.

Visit bit.ly/ttecd to download your free guide.

ABOUT THE AUTHOR

Andrew Gilmore writes for people who crave a deeper relationship with God but might not know where to begin. His aim is to inspire readers to live by faith by tugging at their heartstrings one moment and making them laugh out loud the next. When he's not writing, you can find him eating way too much barbecue, wrestling with his kids, or watching really bad movies. He and his wife, Katie, live in Norman, Oklahoma with their four children. Learn more about Andrew at bit.ly/about-andrew.

Connect with the Author

191

Twitter: @theAndyGilmore
Facebook: facebook.com/andrewgilmorenet